DAILY

CHILDCARE

LOG

DAILY CHILDCARE LOG

SOLIDS: Today I ate ...

Breakfast Time	Lunch Time
I ate _____ of _____	I ate _____ of _____
I ate _____ of _____	I ate _____ of _____
The meal was: □ yummy □ ok □ yucky	The meal was: □ yummy □ ok □ yucky
I drank _____ ozs of water.	I drank _____ ozs of water.

MILK: Today I drank ...

Time: _____ OZ: _____	Time: _____ OZ: _____
Time: _____ OZ: _____	Time: _____ OZ: _____
Time: _____ OZ: _____	Time: _____ OZ: _____

DIAPERS: Today went...

B/M: _____ diapers	Wet: _____ diapers	Combo: _____ diapers

Notes:_____

_____

_____

NAP – TIME: TODAY: Today I slept ...

Start Time: _____	Duration: _____
Start Time: _____	Duration: _____
Start Time: _____	Duration: _____

ACTVITIES: TODAY

Read: _____	□ Went for a walk
Played: _____	□ Went to the Playground
Sung/Danced to: _____	□ Played outside
Learned: _____	□ Watched _____

NOTES

Today my overall mood was: _____

_____

DAILY CHILDCARE LOG

SOLIDS: Today I ate ...

Breakfast Time	Lunch Time
I ate _____ of _____	I ate _____ of _____
I ate _____ of _____	I ate _____ of _____
The meal was: □ yummy □ ok □ yucky	The meal was: □ yummy □ ok □ yucky
I drank _____ ozs of water.	I drank _____ ozs of water.

MILK: Today I drank ...

Time: _____	OZ: _____	Time: _____	OZ: _____
Time: _____	OZ: _____	Time: _____	OZ: _____
Time: _____	OZ: _____	Time: _____	OZ: _____

DIAPERS: Today went...

B/M: _____ diapers	Wet: _____ diapers	Combo: _____ diapers

Notes:_____

_____

_____

NAP – TIME: TODAY: Today I slept ...

Start Time: _____	Duration: _____
Start Time: _____	Duration: _____
Start Time: _____	Duration: _____

ACTVITIES: TODAY

Read: _____	□ Went for a walk
Played: _____	□ Went to the Playground
Sung/Danced to: _____	□ Played outside
Learned: _____	□ Watched _____

NOTES

Today my overall mood was: _____

_____

DAILY CHILDCARE LOG

SOLIDS: Today I ate ...

Breakfast Time	Lunch Time
I ate _____ of _____	I ate _____ of _____
I ate _____ of _____	I ate _____ of _____
The meal was: ☐ yummy ☐ ok ☐ yucky	The meal was: ☐ yummy ☐ ok ☐ yucky
I drank _____ ozs of water.	I drank _____ ozs of water.

MILK: Today I drank ...

Time: _____ OZ: _____	Time: _____ OZ: _____
Time: _____ OZ: _____	Time: _____ OZ: _____
Time: _____ OZ: _____	Time: _____ OZ: _____

DIAPERS: Today went...

B/M: _____ diapers	Wet: _____ diapers	Combo: _____ diapers

Notes:_____

_____

_____

NAP – TIME: TODAY: Today I slept ...

Start Time: _____	Duration: _____
Start Time: _____	Duration: _____
Start Time: _____	Duration: _____

ACTVITIES: TODAY

Read: _____	☐ Went for a walk
Played: _____	☐ Went to the Playground
Sung/Danced to: _____	☐ Played outside
Learned: _____	☐ Watched _____

NOTES

Today my overall mood was: _____

_____

DAILY CHILDCARE LOG

SOLIDS: Today I ate ...

Breakfast Time	Lunch Time
I ate _____ of _____	I ate _____ of _____
I ate _____ of _____	I ate _____ of _____
The meal was: □ yummy □ ok □ yucky	The meal was: □ yummy □ ok □ yucky
I drank _____ ozs of water.	I drank _____ ozs of water.

MILK: Today I drank ...

Time: _____ OZ: _____	Time: _____ OZ: _____
Time: _____ OZ: _____	Time: _____ OZ: _____
Time: _____ OZ: _____	Time: _____ OZ: _____

DIAPERS: Today went...

B/M: _____ diapers	Wet: _____ diapers	Combo: _____ diapers

Notes:_____

_____

_____

NAP – TIME: TODAY: Today I slept ...

Start Time: _____	Duration: _____
Start Time: _____	Duration: _____
Start Time: _____	Duration: _____

ACTVITIES: TODAY

Read: _____	□ Went for a walk
Played: _____	□ Went to the Playground
Sung/Danced to: _____	□ Played outside
Learned: _____	□ Watched _____

NOTES

Today my overall mood was: _____

_____

DAILY CHILDCARE LOG

SOLIDS: Today I ate ...

Breakfast Time	Lunch Time
I ate _____ of _____	I ate _____ of _____
I ate _____ of _____	I ate _____ of _____
The meal was: ☐ yummy ☐ ok ☐ yucky	The meal was: ☐ yummy ☐ ok ☐ yucky
I drank _____ ozs of water.	I drank _____ ozs of water.

MILK: Today I drank ...

Time: _____ OZ: _____	Time: _____ OZ: _____
Time: _____ OZ: _____	Time: _____ OZ: _____
Time: _____ OZ: _____	Time: _____ OZ: _____

DIAPERS: Today went...

B/M: _____ diapers	Wet: _____ diapers	Combo: _____ diapers

Notes:_____

_____

_____

NAP – TIME: TODAY: Today I slept ...

Start Time: _____	Duration: _____
Start Time: _____	Duration: _____
Start Time: _____	Duration: _____

ACTVITIES: TODAY

Read: _____	☐ Went for a walk
Played: _____	☐ Went to the Playground
Sung/Danced to: _____	☐ Played outside
Learned: _____	☐ Watched _____

NOTES

Today my overall mood was: _____

_____

DAILY CHILDCARE LOG

SOLIDS: Today I ate …

Breakfast Time	Lunch Time
I ate _____ of _____	I ate _____ of _____
I ate _____ of _____	I ate _____ of _____
The meal was: ☐ yummy ☐ ok ☐ yucky	The meal was: ☐ yummy ☐ ok ☐ yucky
I drank _____ ozs of water.	I drank _____ ozs of water.

MILK: Today I drank …

Time: _____ OZ: _____	Time: _____ OZ: _____
Time: _____ OZ: _____	Time: _____ OZ: _____
Time: _____ OZ: _____	Time: _____ OZ: _____

DIAPERS: Today went…

B/M: _____ diapers	Wet: _____ diapers	Combo: _____ diapers

Notes:_____

_____

_____

NAP – TIME: TODAY: Today I slept …

Start Time: _____	Duration: _____
Start Time: _____	Duration: _____
Start Time: _____	Duration: _____

ACTVITIES: TODAY

Read: _____	☐ Went for a walk
Played: _____	☐ Went to the Playground
Sung/Danced to: _____	☐ Played outside
Learned: _____	☐ Watched _____

NOTES

Today my overall mood was: _____

_____

DAILY CHILDCARE LOG

SOLIDS: Today I ate ...

Breakfast Time	Lunch Time
I ate _____ of _____	I ate _____ of _____
I ate _____ of _____	I ate _____ of _____
The meal was: ☐ yummy ☐ ok ☐ yucky	The meal was: ☐ yummy ☐ ok ☐ yucky
I drank _____ ozs of water.	I drank _____ ozs of water.

MILK: Today I drank ...

Time: _____ OZ: _____	Time: _____ OZ: _____
Time: _____ OZ: _____	Time: _____ OZ: _____
Time: _____ OZ: _____	Time: _____ OZ: _____

DIAPERS: Today went...

B/M: _____ diapers	Wet: _____ diapers	Combo: _____ diapers

Notes:_____

_____

_____

NAP – TIME: TODAY: Today I slept ...

Start Time: _____	Duration: _____
Start Time: _____	Duration: _____
Start Time: _____	Duration: _____

ACTVITIES: TODAY

Read: _____	☐ Went for a walk
Played: _____	☐ Went to the Playground
Sung/Danced to: _____	☐ Played outside
Learned: _____	☐ Watched _____

NOTES

Today my overall mood was: _____

_____

DAILY CHILDCARE LOG

SOLIDS: Today I ate ...

Breakfast Time	Lunch Time
I ate _____ of _____	I ate _____ of _____
I ate _____ of _____	I ate _____ of _____
The meal was: □ yummy □ ok □ yucky	The meal was: □ yummy □ ok □ yucky
I drank _____ ozs of water.	I drank _____ ozs of water.

MILK: Today I drank ...

Time: _____ OZ: _____	Time: _____ OZ: _____
Time: _____ OZ: _____	Time: _____ OZ: _____
Time: _____ OZ: _____	Time: _____ OZ: _____

DIAPERS: Today went...

B/M: _____ diapers	Wet: _____ diapers	Combo: _____ diapers

Notes:_____

_____

_____

NAP – TIME: TODAY: Today I slept ...

Start Time: _____	Duration: _____
Start Time: _____	Duration: _____
Start Time: _____	Duration: _____

ACTVITIES: TODAY

Read: _____	□ Went for a walk
Played: _____	□ Went to the Playground
Sung/Danced to: _____	□ Played outside
Learned: _____	□ Watched _____

NOTES

Today my overall mood was: _____

_____

DAILY CHILDCARE LOG

SOLIDS: Today I ate ...

Breakfast Time	Lunch Time
I ate _____ of _____	I ate _____ of _____
I ate _____ of _____	I ate _____ of _____
The meal was: □ yummy □ ok □ yucky	The meal was: □ yummy □ ok □ yucky
I drank _____ ozs of water.	I drank _____ ozs of water.

MILK: Today I drank ...

Time: _____ OZ: _____	Time: _____ OZ: _____
Time: _____ OZ: _____	Time: _____ OZ: _____
Time: _____ OZ: _____	Time: _____ OZ: _____

DIAPERS: Today went...

B/M: _____ diapers	Wet: _____ diapers	Combo: _____ diapers

Notes:_____

_____

_____

NAP – TIME: TODAY: Today I slept ...

Start Time: _____	Duration: _____
Start Time: _____	Duration: _____
Start Time: _____	Duration: _____

ACTVITIES: TODAY

Read: _____	□ Went for a walk
Played: _____	□ Went to the Playground
Sung/Danced to: _____	□ Played outside
Learned: _____	□ Watched _____

NOTES

Today my overall mood was: _____

_____

DAILY CHILDCARE LOG

SOLIDS: Today I ate ...

Breakfast Time	Lunch Time
I ate _____ of _____	I ate _____ of _____
I ate _____ of _____	I ate _____ of _____
The meal was: □ yummy □ ok □ yucky	The meal was: □ yummy □ ok □ yucky
I drank _____ ozs of water.	I drank _____ ozs of water.

MILK: Today I drank ...

Time: _____ OZ: _____	Time: _____ OZ: _____
Time: _____ OZ: _____	Time: _____ OZ: _____
Time: _____ OZ: _____	Time: _____ OZ: _____

DIAPERS: Today went...

B/M: _____ diapers	Wet: _____ diapers	Combo: _____ diapers

Notes:_____

_____

_____

NAP – TIME: TODAY: Today I slept ...

Start Time: _____	Duration: _____
Start Time: _____	Duration: _____
Start Time: _____	Duration: _____

ACTVITIES: TODAY

Read: _____	□ Went for a walk
Played: _____	□ Went to the Playground
Sung/Danced to: _____	□ Played outside
Learned: _____	□ Watched _____

NOTES

Today my overall mood was: _____

_____

DAILY CHILDCARE LOG

SOLIDS: Today I ate ...

Breakfast Time	Lunch Time
I ate _____ of _____	I ate _____ of _____
I ate _____ of _____	I ate _____ of _____
The meal was: □ yummy □ ok □ yucky	The meal was: □ yummy □ ok □ yucky
I drank _____ ozs of water.	I drank _____ ozs of water.

MILK: Today I drank ...

Time: _____	OZ: _____	Time: _____	OZ: _____
Time: _____	OZ: _____	Time: _____	OZ: _____
Time: _____	OZ: _____	Time: _____	OZ: _____

DIAPERS: Today went...

B/M: _____ diapers	Wet: _____ diapers	Combo: _____ diapers

Notes:_____

_____

_____

NAP – TIME: TODAY: Today I slept ...

Start Time: _____	Duration: _____
Start Time: _____	Duration: _____
Start Time: _____	Duration: _____

ACTVITIES: TODAY

Read: _____	□ Went for a walk
Played: _____	□ Went to the Playground
Sung/Danced to: _____	□ Played outside
Learned: _____	□ Watched _____

NOTES

Today my overall mood was: _____

_____

DAILY CHILDCARE LOG

SOLIDS: Today I ate ...

Breakfast Time	Lunch Time
I ate _____ of _____	I ate _____ of _____
I ate _____ of _____	I ate _____ of _____
The meal was: □ yummy □ ok □ yucky	The meal was: □ yummy □ ok □ yucky
I drank _____ ozs of water.	I drank _____ ozs of water.

MILK: Today I drank ...

Time: _____ OZ: _____	Time: _____ OZ: _____
Time: _____ OZ: _____	Time: _____ OZ: _____
Time: _____ OZ: _____	Time: _____ OZ: _____

DIAPERS: Today went...

B/M: _____ diapers	Wet: _____ diapers	Combo: _____ diapers

Notes:_____

_____

_____

NAP – TIME: TODAY: Today I slept ...

Start Time: _____	Duration: _____
Start Time: _____	Duration: _____
Start Time: _____	Duration: _____

ACTVITIES: TODAY

Read: _____	□ Went for a walk
Played: _____	□ Went to the Playground
Sung/Danced to: _____	□ Played outside
Learned: _____	□ Watched _____

NOTES

Today my overall mood was: _____

_____

DAILY CHILDCARE LOG

SOLIDS: Today I ate …

Breakfast Time	Lunch Time
I ate _____ of _____	I ate _____ of _____
I ate _____ of _____	I ate _____ of _____
The meal was: □ yummy □ ok □ yucky	The meal was: □ yummy □ ok □ yucky
I drank _____ ozs of water.	I drank _____ ozs of water.

MILK: Today I drank …

Time: _____	OZ: _____	Time: _____	OZ: _____
Time: _____	OZ: _____	Time: _____	OZ: _____
Time: _____	OZ: _____	Time: _____	OZ: _____

DIAPERS: Today went…

B/M: _____ diapers	Wet: _____ diapers	Combo: _____ diapers

Notes:_____

_____

_____

NAP – TIME: TODAY: Today I slept …

Start Time: _____	Duration: _____
Start Time: _____	Duration: _____
Start Time: _____	Duration: _____

ACTVITIES: TODAY

Read: _____	□ Went for a walk
Played: _____	□ Went to the Playground
Sung/Danced to: _____	□ Played outside
Learned: _____	□ Watched _____

NOTES

Today my overall mood was: _____

_____

DAILY CHILDCARE LOG

SOLIDS: Today I ate ...

Breakfast Time	Lunch Time
I ate _____ of _____	I ate _____ of _____
I ate _____ of _____	I ate _____ of _____
The meal was: ☐ yummy ☐ ok ☐ yucky	The meal was: ☐ yummy ☐ ok ☐ yucky
I drank _____ ozs of water.	I drank _____ ozs of water.

MILK: Today I drank ...

Time: _____ OZ: _____	Time: _____ OZ: _____
Time: _____ OZ: _____	Time: _____ OZ: _____
Time: _____ OZ: _____	Time: _____ OZ: _____

DIAPERS: Today went...

B/M: _____ diapers	Wet: _____ diapers	Combo: _____ diapers

Notes:_____

_____

_____

NAP – TIME: TODAY: Today I slept ...

Start Time: _____	Duration: _____
Start Time: _____	Duration: _____
Start Time: _____	Duration: _____

ACTVITIES: TODAY

Read: _____	☐ Went for a walk
Played: _____	☐ Went to the Playground
Sung/Danced to: _____	☐ Played outside
Learned: _____	☐ Watched _____

NOTES

Today my overall mood was: _____

_____

DAILY CHILDCARE LOG

SOLIDS: Today I ate ...

Breakfast Time	Lunch Time
I ate _____ of _____	I ate _____ of _____
I ate _____ of _____	I ate _____ of _____
The meal was: □ yummy □ ok □ yucky	The meal was: □ yummy □ ok □ yucky
I drank _____ ozs of water.	I drank _____ ozs of water.

MILK: Today I drank ...

Time: _____ OZ: _____	Time: _____ OZ: _____
Time: _____ OZ: _____	Time: _____ OZ: _____
Time: _____ OZ: _____	Time: _____ OZ: _____

DIAPERS: Today went...

B/M: _____ diapers	Wet: _____ diapers	Combo: _____ diapers

Notes:_____

_____

_____

NAP – TIME: TODAY: Today I slept ...

Start Time: _____	Duration: _____
Start Time: _____	Duration: _____
Start Time: _____	Duration: _____

ACTVITIES: TODAY

Read: _____	□ Went for a walk
Played: _____	□ Went to the Playground
Sung/Danced to: _____	□ Played outside
Learned: _____	□ Watched _____

NOTES

Today my overall mood was: _____

_____

DAILY CHILDCARE LOG

SOLIDS: Today I ate ...

Breakfast Time	Lunch Time
I ate _____ of _____	I ate _____ of _____
I ate _____ of _____	I ate _____ of _____
The meal was: □ yummy □ ok □ yucky	The meal was: □ yummy □ ok □ yucky
I drank _____ ozs of water.	I drank _____ ozs of water.

MILK: Today I drank ...

Time: _____ OZ: _____	Time: _____ OZ: _____
Time: _____ OZ: _____	Time: _____ OZ: _____
Time: _____ OZ: _____	Time: _____ OZ: _____

DIAPERS: Today went...

B/M: _____ diapers	Wet: _____ diapers	Combo: _____ diapers

Notes:_____

_____

_____

NAP – TIME: TODAY: Today I slept ...

Start Time: _____	Duration: _____
Start Time: _____	Duration: _____
Start Time: _____	Duration: _____

ACTVITIES: TODAY

Read: _____	□ Went for a walk
Played: _____	□ Went to the Playground
Sung/Danced to: _____	□ Played outside
Learned: _____	□ Watched _____

NOTES

Today my overall mood was: _____

_____

DAILY CHILDCARE LOG

SOLIDS: Today I ate ...

Breakfast Time	Lunch Time
I ate _____ of _____	I ate _____ of _____
I ate _____ of _____	I ate _____ of _____
The meal was: ☐ yummy ☐ ok ☐ yucky	The meal was: ☐ yummy ☐ ok ☐ yucky
I drank _____ ozs of water.	I drank _____ ozs of water.

MILK: Today I drank ...

Time: _____ OZ: _____	Time: _____ OZ: _____
Time: _____ OZ: _____	Time: _____ OZ: _____
Time: _____ OZ: _____	Time: _____ OZ: _____

DIAPERS: Today went...

B/M: _____ diapers	Wet: _____ diapers	Combo: _____ diapers

Notes:_____

_____

_____

NAP – TIME: TODAY: Today I slept ...

Start Time: _____	Duration: _____
Start Time: _____	Duration: _____
Start Time: _____	Duration: _____

ACTVITIES: TODAY

Read: _____	☐ Went for a walk
Played: _____	☐ Went to the Playground
Sung/Danced to: _____	☐ Played outside
Learned: _____	☐ Watched _____

NOTES

Today my overall mood was: _____

_____

DAILY CHILDCARE LOG

SOLIDS: Today I ate ...

Breakfast Time	Lunch Time
I ate _____ of _____	I ate _____ of _____
I ate _____ of _____	I ate _____ of _____
The meal was: □ yummy □ ok □ yucky	The meal was: □ yummy □ ok □ yucky
I drank _____ ozs of water.	I drank _____ ozs of water.

MILK: Today I drank ...

Time: _____ OZ: _____	Time: _____ OZ: _____
Time: _____ OZ: _____	Time: _____ OZ: _____
Time: _____ OZ: _____	Time: _____ OZ: _____

DIAPERS: Today went...

B/M: _____ diapers	Wet: _____ diapers	Combo: _____ diapers

Notes:_____

_____

_____

NAP – TIME: TODAY: Today I slept ...

Start Time: _____	Duration: _____
Start Time: _____	Duration: _____
Start Time: _____	Duration: _____

ACTVITIES: TODAY

Read: _____	□ Went for a walk
Played: _____	□ Went to the Playground
Sung/Danced to: _____	□ Played outside
Learned: _____	□ Watched _____

NOTES

Today my overall mood was: _____

_____

DAILY CHILDCARE LOG

SOLIDS: Today I ate ...

Breakfast Time	Lunch Time
I ate _____ of _____	I ate _____ of _____
I ate _____ of _____	I ate _____ of _____
The meal was: □ yummy □ ok □ yucky	The meal was: □ yummy □ ok □ yucky
I drank _____ ozs of water.	I drank _____ ozs of water.

MILK: Today I drank ...

Time: _____ OZ: _____	Time: _____ OZ: _____
Time: _____ OZ: _____	Time: _____ OZ: _____
Time: _____ OZ: _____	Time: _____ OZ: _____

DIAPERS: Today went...

B/M: _____ diapers	Wet: _____ diapers	Combo: _____ diapers

Notes:_____

_____

_____

NAP – TIME: TODAY: Today I slept ...

Start Time: _____	Duration: _____
Start Time: _____	Duration: _____
Start Time: _____	Duration: _____

ACTVITIES: TODAY

Read: _____	□ Went for a walk
Played: _____	□ Went to the Playground
Sung/Danced to: _____	□ Played outside
Learned: _____	□ Watched _____

NOTES

Today my overall mood was: _____

_____

DAILY CHILDCARE LOG

SOLIDS: Today I ate ...

Breakfast Time	Lunch Time
I ate _____ of _____	I ate _____ of _____
I ate _____ of _____	I ate _____ of _____
The meal was: □ yummy □ ok □ yucky	The meal was: □ yummy □ ok □ yucky
I drank _____ ozs of water.	I drank _____ ozs of water.

MILK: Today I drank ...

Time: _____ OZ: _____	Time: _____ OZ: _____
Time: _____ OZ: _____	Time: _____ OZ: _____
Time: _____ OZ: _____	Time: _____ OZ: _____

DIAPERS: Today went...

B/M: _____ diapers	Wet: _____ diapers	Combo: _____ diapers

Notes:_____
_____
_____

NAP – TIME: TODAY: Today I slept ...

Start Time: _____	Duration: _____
Start Time: _____	Duration: _____
Start Time: _____	Duration: _____

ACTVITIES: TODAY

Read: _____	□ Went for a walk
Played: _____	□ Went to the Playground
Sung/Danced to: _____	□ Played outside
Learned: _____	□ Watched _____

NOTES

Today my overall mood was: _____
_____

DAILY CHILDCARE LOG

SOLIDS: Today I ate ...

Breakfast Time	Lunch Time
I ate _____ of _____	I ate _____ of _____
I ate _____ of _____	I ate _____ of _____
The meal was: □ yummy □ ok □ yucky	The meal was: □ yummy □ ok □ yucky
I drank _____ ozs of water.	I drank _____ ozs of water.

MILK: Today I drank ...

Time: _____ OZ: _____	Time: _____ OZ: _____
Time: _____ OZ: _____	Time: _____ OZ: _____
Time: _____ OZ: _____	Time: _____ OZ: _____

DIAPERS: Today went...

B/M: _____ diapers	Wet: _____ diapers	Combo: _____ diapers

Notes:_____

_____

_____

NAP – TIME: TODAY: Today I slept ...

Start Time: _____	Duration: _____
Start Time: _____	Duration: _____
Start Time: _____	Duration: _____

ACTVITIES: TODAY

Read: _____	□ Went for a walk
Played: _____	□ Went to the Playground
Sung/Danced to: _____	□ Played outside
Learned: _____	□ Watched _____

NOTES

Today my overall mood was: _____

_____

DAILY CHILDCARE LOG

SOLIDS: Today I ate …

Breakfast Time	Lunch Time
I ate _____ of _____	I ate _____ of _____
I ate _____ of _____	I ate _____ of _____
The meal was: □ yummy □ ok □ yucky	The meal was: □ yummy □ ok □ yucky
I drank _____ ozs of water.	I drank _____ ozs of water.

MILK: Today I drank …

Time: _____ OZ: _____	Time: _____ OZ: _____
Time: _____ OZ: _____	Time: _____ OZ: _____
Time: _____ OZ: _____	Time: _____ OZ: _____

DIAPERS: Today went…

B/M: _____ diapers	Wet: _____ diapers	Combo: _____ diapers

Notes:_____

_____

_____

NAP – TIME: TODAY: Today I slept …

Start Time: _____	Duration: _____
Start Time: _____	Duration: _____
Start Time: _____	Duration: _____

ACTVITIES: TODAY

Read: _____	□ Went for a walk
Played: _____	□ Went to the Playground
Sung/Danced to: _____	□ Played outside
Learned: _____	□ Watched _____

NOTES

Today my overall mood was: _____

_____

DAILY CHILDCARE LOG

SOLIDS: Today I ate ...

Breakfast Time	Lunch Time
I ate _____ of _____	I ate _____ of _____
I ate _____ of _____	I ate _____ of _____
The meal was: □ yummy □ ok □ yucky	The meal was: □ yummy □ ok □ yucky
I drank _____ ozs of water.	I drank _____ ozs of water.

MILK: Today I drank ...

Time: _____ OZ: _____	Time: _____ OZ: _____
Time: _____ OZ: _____	Time: _____ OZ: _____
Time: _____ OZ: _____	Time: _____ OZ: _____

DIAPERS: Today went...

B/M: _____ diapers	Wet: _____ diapers	Combo: _____ diapers

Notes:_____

_____

_____

NAP – TIME: TODAY: Today I slept ...

Start Time: _____	Duration: _____
Start Time: _____	Duration: _____
Start Time: _____	Duration: _____

ACTVITIES: TODAY

Read: _____	□ Went for a walk
Played: _____	□ Went to the Playground
Sung/Danced to: _____	□ Played outside
Learned: _____	□ Watched _____

NOTES

Today my overall mood was: _____

_____

DAILY CHILDCARE LOG

SOLIDS: Today I ate …

Breakfast Time	Lunch Time
I ate _____ of _____	I ate _____ of _____
I ate _____ of _____	I ate _____ of _____
The meal was: □ yummy □ ok □ yucky	The meal was: □ yummy □ ok □ yucky
I drank _____ ozs of water.	I drank _____ ozs of water.

MILK: Today I drank …

Time: _____	OZ: _____	Time: _____	OZ: _____
Time: _____	OZ: _____	Time: _____	OZ: _____
Time: _____	OZ: _____	Time: _____	OZ: _____

DIAPERS: Today went…

B/M: _____ diapers	Wet: _____ diapers	Combo: _____ diapers

Notes:_____

_____

_____

NAP – TIME: TODAY: Today I slept …

Start Time: _____	Duration: _____
Start Time: _____	Duration: _____
Start Time: _____	Duration: _____

ACTVITIES: TODAY

Read: _____	□ Went for a walk
Played: _____	□ Went to the Playground
Sung/Danced to: _____	□ Played outside
Learned: _____	□ Watched _____

NOTES

Today my overall mood was: _____

_____

DAILY CHILDCARE LOG

SOLIDS: Today I ate ...

Breakfast Time	Lunch Time
I ate _____ of _____	I ate _____ of _____
I ate _____ of _____	I ate _____ of _____
The meal was: □ yummy □ ok □ yucky	The meal was: □ yummy □ ok □ yucky
I drank _____ ozs of water.	I drank _____ ozs of water.

MILK: Today I drank ...

Time: _____ OZ: _____	Time: _____ OZ: _____
Time: _____ OZ: _____	Time: _____ OZ: _____
Time: _____ OZ: _____	Time: _____ OZ: _____

DIAPERS: Today went...

B/M: _____ diapers	Wet: _____ diapers	Combo: _____ diapers

Notes:_____

_____

_____

NAP – TIME: TODAY: Today I slept ...

Start Time: _____	Duration: _____
Start Time: _____	Duration: _____
Start Time: _____	Duration: _____

ACTVITIES: TODAY

Read: _____	□ Went for a walk
Played: _____	□ Went to the Playground
Sung/Danced to: _____	□ Played outside
Learned: _____	□ Watched _____

NOTES

Today my overall mood was: _____

_____

DAILY CHILDCARE LOG

SOLIDS: Today I ate ...

Breakfast Time	Lunch Time
I ate _____ of _____	I ate _____ of _____
I ate _____ of _____	I ate _____ of _____
The meal was: □ yummy □ ok □ yucky	The meal was: □ yummy □ ok □ yucky
I drank _____ ozs of water.	I drank _____ ozs of water.

MILK: Today I drank ...

Time: _____ OZ: _____	Time: _____ OZ: _____
Time: _____ OZ: _____	Time: _____ OZ: _____
Time: _____ OZ: _____	Time: _____ OZ: _____

DIAPERS: Today went...

B/M: _____ diapers	Wet: _____ diapers	Combo: _____ diapers

Notes:_____

_____

_____

NAP – TIME: TODAY: Today I slept ...

Start Time: _____	Duration: _____
Start Time: _____	Duration: _____
Start Time: _____	Duration: _____

ACTVITIES: TODAY

Read: _____	□ Went for a walk
Played: _____	□ Went to the Playground
Sung/Danced to: _____	□ Played outside
Learned: _____	□ Watched _____

NOTES

Today my overall mood was: _____

_____

DAILY CHILDCARE LOG

SOLIDS: Today I ate ...

Breakfast Time	Lunch Time
I ate _____ of _____	I ate _____ of _____
I ate _____ of _____	I ate _____ of _____
The meal was: □ yummy □ ok □ yucky	The meal was: □ yummy □ ok □ yucky
I drank _____ ozs of water.	I drank _____ ozs of water.

MILK: Today I drank ...

Time: _____	OZ: _____	Time: _____	OZ: _____
Time: _____	OZ: _____	Time: _____	OZ: _____
Time: _____	OZ: _____	Time: _____	OZ: _____

DIAPERS: Today went...

B/M: _____ diapers	Wet: _____ diapers	Combo: _____ diapers

Notes:_____

_____

_____

NAP – TIME: TODAY: Today I slept ...

Start Time: _____	Duration: _____
Start Time: _____	Duration: _____
Start Time: _____	Duration: _____

ACTVITIES: TODAY

Read: _____	□ Went for a walk
Played: _____	□ Went to the Playground
Sung/Danced to: _____	□ Played outside
Learned: _____	□ Watched _____

NOTES

Today my overall mood was: _____

_____

DAILY CHILDCARE LOG

SOLIDS: Today I ate ...

Breakfast Time	Lunch Time
I ate _____ of _____	I ate _____ of _____
I ate _____ of _____	I ate _____ of _____
The meal was: □ yummy □ ok □ yucky	The meal was: □ yummy □ ok □ yucky
I drank _____ ozs of water.	I drank _____ ozs of water.

MILK: Today I drank ...

Time: _____ OZ: _____	Time: _____ OZ: _____
Time: _____ OZ: _____	Time: _____ OZ: _____
Time: _____ OZ: _____	Time: _____ OZ: _____

DIAPERS: Today went...

B/M: _____ diapers	Wet: _____ diapers	Combo: _____ diapers

Notes:_____

_____

_____

NAP – TIME: TODAY: Today I slept ...

Start Time: _____	Duration: _____
Start Time: _____	Duration: _____
Start Time: _____	Duration: _____

ACTVITIES: TODAY

Read: _____	□ Went for a walk
Played: _____	□ Went to the Playground
Sung/Danced to: _____	□ Played outside
Learned: _____	□ Watched _____

NOTES

Today my overall mood was: _____

_____

DAILY CHILDCARE LOG

SOLIDS: Today I ate ...

Breakfast Time	Lunch Time
I ate _____ of _____	I ate _____ of _____
I ate _____ of _____	I ate _____ of _____
The meal was: ☐ yummy ☐ ok ☐ yucky	The meal was: ☐ yummy ☐ ok ☐ yucky
I drank _____ ozs of water.	I drank _____ ozs of water.

MILK: Today I drank ...

Time: _____ OZ: _____	Time: _____ OZ: _____
Time: _____ OZ: _____	Time: _____ OZ: _____
Time: _____ OZ: _____	Time: _____ OZ: _____

DIAPERS: Today went...

B/M: _____ diapers	Wet: _____ diapers	Combo: _____ diapers

Notes:_____

_____

_____

NAP – TIME: TODAY: Today I slept ...

Start Time: _____	Duration: _____
Start Time: _____	Duration: _____
Start Time: _____	Duration: _____

ACTVITIES: TODAY

Read: _____	☐ Went for a walk
Played: _____	☐ Went to the Playground
Sung/Danced to: _____	☐ Played outside
Learned: _____	☐ Watched _____

NOTES

Today my overall mood was: _____

_____

DAILY CHILDCARE LOG

SOLIDS: Today I ate ...

Breakfast Time	Lunch Time
I ate _____ of _____	I ate _____ of _____
I ate _____ of _____	I ate _____ of _____
The meal was: □ yummy □ ok □ yucky	The meal was: □ yummy □ ok □ yucky
I drank _____ ozs of water.	I drank _____ ozs of water.

MILK: Today I drank ...

Time: _____ OZ: _____	Time: _____ OZ: _____
Time: _____ OZ: _____	Time: _____ OZ: _____
Time: _____ OZ: _____	Time: _____ OZ: _____

DIAPERS: Today went...

B/M: _____ diapers	Wet: _____ diapers	Combo: _____ diapers

Notes:_____

_____

_____

NAP – TIME: TODAY: Today I slept ...

Start Time: _____	Duration: _____
Start Time: _____	Duration: _____
Start Time: _____	Duration: _____

ACTVITIES: TODAY

Read: _____	□ Went for a walk
Played: _____	□ Went to the Playground
Sung/Danced to: _____	□ Played outside
Learned: _____	□ Watched _____

NOTES

Today my overall mood was: _____

_____

DAILY CHILDCARE LOG

SOLIDS: Today I ate ...

Breakfast Time	Lunch Time
I ate _____ of _____	I ate _____ of _____
I ate _____ of _____	I ate _____ of _____
The meal was: □ yummy □ ok □ yucky	The meal was: □ yummy □ ok □ yucky
I drank _____ ozs of water.	I drank _____ ozs of water.

MILK: Today I drank ...

Time: _____ OZ: _____	Time: _____ OZ: _____
Time: _____ OZ: _____	Time: _____ OZ: _____
Time: _____ OZ: _____	Time: _____ OZ: _____

DIAPERS: Today went...

B/M: _____ diapers	Wet: _____ diapers	Combo: _____ diapers

Notes:_____

_____

_____

NAP – TIME: TODAY: Today I slept ...

Start Time: _____	Duration: _____
Start Time: _____	Duration: _____
Start Time: _____	Duration: _____

ACTVITIES: TODAY

Read: _____	□ Went for a walk
Played: _____	□ Went to the Playground
Sung/Danced to: _____	□ Played outside
Learned: _____	□ Watched _____

NOTES

Today my overall mood was: _____

_____

DAILY CHILDCARE LOG

SOLIDS: Today I ate ...

Breakfast Time	Lunch Time
I ate _____ of _____	I ate _____ of _____
I ate _____ of _____	I ate _____ of _____
The meal was: □ yummy □ ok □ yucky	The meal was: □ yummy □ ok □ yucky
I drank _____ ozs of water.	I drank _____ ozs of water.

MILK: Today I drank ...

Time: _____ OZ: _____	Time: _____ OZ: _____
Time: _____ OZ: _____	Time: _____ OZ: _____
Time: _____ OZ: _____	Time: _____ OZ: _____

DIAPERS: Today went...

B/M: _____ diapers	Wet: _____ diapers	Combo: _____ diapers

Notes:_____

_____

_____

NAP – TIME: TODAY: Today I slept ...

Start Time: _____	Duration: _____
Start Time: _____	Duration: _____
Start Time: _____	Duration: _____

ACTVITIES: TODAY

Read: _____	□ Went for a walk
Played: _____	□ Went to the Playground
Sung/Danced to: _____	□ Played outside
Learned: _____	□ Watched _____

NOTES

Today my overall mood was: _____

_____

DAILY CHILDCARE LOG

SOLIDS: Today I ate ...

Breakfast Time	Lunch Time
I ate _____ of _____	I ate _____ of _____
I ate _____ of _____	I ate _____ of _____
The meal was: □ yummy □ ok □ yucky	The meal was: □ yummy □ ok □ yucky
I drank _____ ozs of water.	I drank _____ ozs of water.

MILK: Today I drank ...

Time: _____ OZ: _____	Time: _____ OZ: _____
Time: _____ OZ: _____	Time: _____ OZ: _____
Time: _____ OZ: _____	Time: _____ OZ: _____

DIAPERS: Today went...

B/M: _____ diapers	Wet: _____ diapers	Combo: _____ diapers

Notes:_____

_____

_____

NAP – TIME: TODAY: Today I slept ...

Start Time: _____	Duration: _____
Start Time: _____	Duration: _____
Start Time: _____	Duration: _____

ACTVITIES: TODAY

Read: _____	□ Went for a walk
Played: _____	□ Went to the Playground
Sung/Danced to: _____	□ Played outside
Learned: _____	□ Watched _____

NOTES

Today my overall mood was: _____

_____

DAILY CHILDCARE LOG

SOLIDS: Today I ate …

Breakfast Time	Lunch Time
I ate _____ of _____	I ate _____ of _____
I ate _____ of _____	I ate _____ of _____
The meal was: □ yummy □ ok □ yucky	The meal was: □ yummy □ ok □ yucky
I drank _____ ozs of water.	I drank _____ ozs of water.

MILK: Today I drank …

Time: _____ OZ: _____	Time: _____ OZ: _____
Time: _____ OZ: _____	Time: _____ OZ: _____
Time: _____ OZ: _____	Time: _____ OZ: _____

DIAPERS: Today went…

B/M: _____ diapers	Wet: _____ diapers	Combo: _____ diapers

Notes:_____

_____

_____

NAP – TIME: TODAY: Today I slept …

Start Time: _____	Duration: _____
Start Time: _____	Duration: _____
Start Time: _____	Duration: _____

ACTVITIES: TODAY

Read: _____	□ Went for a walk
Played: _____	□ Went to the Playground
Sung/Danced to: _____	□ Played outside
Learned: _____	□ Watched _____

NOTES

Today my overall mood was: _____

_____

DAILY CHILDCARE LOG

SOLIDS: Today I ate ...

Breakfast Time	Lunch Time
I ate _____ of _____	I ate _____ of _____
I ate _____ of _____	I ate _____ of _____
The meal was: □ yummy □ ok □ yucky	The meal was: □ yummy □ ok □ yucky
I drank _____ ozs of water.	I drank _____ ozs of water.

MILK: Today I drank ...

Time: _____ OZ: _____	Time: _____ OZ: _____
Time: _____ OZ: _____	Time: _____ OZ: _____
Time: _____ OZ: _____	Time: _____ OZ: _____

DIAPERS: Today went...

B/M: _____ diapers	Wet: _____ diapers	Combo: _____ diapers

Notes:_____

_____

_____

NAP – TIME: TODAY: Today I slept ...

Start Time: _____	Duration: _____
Start Time: _____	Duration: _____
Start Time: _____	Duration: _____

ACTVITIES: TODAY

Read: _____	□ Went for a walk
Played: _____	□ Went to the Playground
Sung/Danced to: _____	□ Played outside
Learned: _____	□ Watched _____

NOTES

Today my overall mood was: _____

_____

DAILY CHILDCARE LOG

SOLIDS: Today I ate ...

Breakfast Time	Lunch Time
I ate _____ of _____	I ate _____ of _____
I ate _____ of _____	I ate _____ of _____
The meal was: □ yummy □ ok □ yucky	The meal was: □ yummy □ ok □ yucky
I drank _____ ozs of water.	I drank _____ ozs of water.

MILK: Today I drank ...

Time: _____ OZ: _____	Time: _____ OZ: _____
Time: _____ OZ: _____	Time: _____ OZ: _____
Time: _____ OZ: _____	Time: _____ OZ: _____

DIAPERS: Today went...

B/M: _____ diapers	Wet: _____ diapers	Combo: _____ diapers

Notes:_____

_____

_____

NAP – TIME: TODAY: Today I slept ...

Start Time: _____	Duration: _____
Start Time: _____	Duration: _____
Start Time: _____	Duration: _____

ACTVITIES: TODAY

Read: _____	□ Went for a walk
Played: _____	□ Went to the Playground
Sung/Danced to: _____	□ Played outside
Learned: _____	□ Watched _____

NOTES

Today my overall mood was: _____

_____

DAILY CHILDCARE LOG

SOLIDS: Today I ate ...

Breakfast Time	Lunch Time
I ate _____ of _____	I ate _____ of _____
I ate _____ of _____	I ate _____ of _____
The meal was: □ yummy □ ok □ yucky	The meal was: □ yummy □ ok □ yucky
I drank _____ ozs of water.	I drank _____ ozs of water.

MILK: Today I drank ...

Time: _____ OZ: _____	Time: _____ OZ: _____
Time: _____ OZ: _____	Time: _____ OZ: _____
Time: _____ OZ: _____	Time: _____ OZ: _____

DIAPERS: Today went...

B/M: _____ diapers	Wet: _____ diapers	Combo: _____ diapers

Notes:_____

_____

_____

NAP – TIME: TODAY: Today I slept ...

Start Time: _____	Duration: _____
Start Time: _____	Duration: _____
Start Time: _____	Duration: _____

ACTVITIES: TODAY

Read: _____	□ Went for a walk
Played: _____	□ Went to the Playground
Sung/Danced to: _____	□ Played outside
Learned: _____	□ Watched _____

NOTES

Today my overall mood was: _____

_____

DAILY CHILDCARE LOG

SOLIDS: Today I ate ...

Breakfast Time	Lunch Time
I ate _____ of _____	I ate _____ of _____
I ate _____ of _____	I ate _____ of _____
The meal was: □ yummy □ ok □ yucky	The meal was: □ yummy □ ok □ yucky
I drank _____ ozs of water.	I drank _____ ozs of water.

MILK: Today I drank ...

Time: _____ OZ: _____	Time: _____ OZ: _____
Time: _____ OZ: _____	Time: _____ OZ: _____
Time: _____ OZ: _____	Time: _____ OZ: _____

DIAPERS: Today went...

B/M: _____ diapers	Wet: _____ diapers	Combo: _____ diapers

Notes:_____

_____

_____

NAP – TIME: TODAY: Today I slept ...

Start Time: _____	Duration: _____
Start Time: _____	Duration: _____
Start Time: _____	Duration: _____

ACTVITIES: TODAY

Read: _____	□ Went for a walk
Played: _____	□ Went to the Playground
Sung/Danced to: _____	□ Played outside
Learned: _____	□ Watched _____

NOTES

Today my overall mood was: _____

_____

DAILY CHILDCARE LOG

SOLIDS: Today I ate …

Breakfast Time	Lunch Time
I ate _____ of _____	I ate _____ of _____
I ate _____ of _____	I ate _____ of _____
The meal was: □ yummy □ ok □ yucky	The meal was: □ yummy □ ok □ yucky
I drank _____ ozs of water.	I drank _____ ozs of water.

MILK: Today I drank …

Time: _____ OZ: _____	Time: _____ OZ: _____
Time: _____ OZ: _____	Time: _____ OZ: _____
Time: _____ OZ: _____	Time: _____ OZ: _____

DIAPERS: Today went…

B/M: _____ diapers	Wet: _____ diapers	Combo: _____ diapers

Notes:_____
_____
_____

NAP – TIME: TODAY: Today I slept …

Start Time: _____	Duration: _____
Start Time: _____	Duration: _____
Start Time: _____	Duration: _____

ACTVITIES: TODAY

Read: _____	□ Went for a walk
Played: _____	□ Went to the Playground
Sung/Danced to: _____	□ Played outside
Learned: _____	□ Watched _____

NOTES

Today my overall mood was: _____
_____

DAILY CHILDCARE LOG

SOLIDS: Today I ate ...

Breakfast Time	Lunch Time
I ate _____ of _____	I ate _____ of _____
I ate _____ of _____	I ate _____ of _____
The meal was: □ yummy □ ok □ yucky	The meal was: □ yummy □ ok □ yucky
I drank _____ ozs of water.	I drank _____ ozs of water.

MILK: Today I drank ...

Time: _____ OZ: _____	Time: _____ OZ: _____
Time: _____ OZ: _____	Time: _____ OZ: _____
Time: _____ OZ: _____	Time: _____ OZ: _____

DIAPERS: Today went...

B/M: _____ diapers	Wet: _____ diapers	Combo: _____ diapers

Notes:_____

_____

_____

NAP – TIME: TODAY: Today I slept ...

Start Time: _____	Duration: _____
Start Time: _____	Duration: _____
Start Time: _____	Duration: _____

ACTVITIES: TODAY

Read: _____	□ Went for a walk
Played: _____	□ Went to the Playground
Sung/Danced to: _____	□ Played outside
Learned: _____	□ Watched _____

NOTES

Today my overall mood was: _____

_____

DAILY CHILDCARE LOG

SOLIDS: Today I ate ...

Breakfast Time	Lunch Time
I ate _____ of _____	I ate _____ of _____
I ate _____ of _____	I ate _____ of _____
The meal was: □ yummy □ ok □ yucky	The meal was: □ yummy □ ok □ yucky
I drank _____ ozs of water.	I drank _____ ozs of water.

MILK: Today I drank ...

Time: _____ OZ: _____	Time: _____ OZ: _____
Time: _____ OZ: _____	Time: _____ OZ: _____
Time: _____ OZ: _____	Time: _____ OZ: _____

DIAPERS: Today went...

B/M: _____ diapers	Wet: _____ diapers	Combo: _____ diapers

Notes:_____
_____
_____

NAP – TIME: TODAY: Today I slept ...

Start Time: _____	Duration: _____
Start Time: _____	Duration: _____
Start Time: _____	Duration: _____

ACTVITIES: TODAY

Read: _____	□ Went for a walk
Played: _____	□ Went to the Playground
Sung/Danced to: _____	□ Played outside
Learned: _____	□ Watched _____

NOTES

Today my overall mood was: _____
_____

DAILY CHILDCARE LOG

SOLIDS: Today I ate ...

Breakfast Time	Lunch Time
I ate _____ of _____	I ate _____ of _____
I ate _____ of _____	I ate _____ of _____
The meal was: □ yummy □ ok □ yucky	The meal was: □ yummy □ ok □ yucky
I drank _____ ozs of water.	I drank _____ ozs of water.

MILK: Today I drank ...

Time: _____ OZ: _____	Time: _____ OZ: _____
Time: _____ OZ: _____	Time: _____ OZ: _____
Time: _____ OZ: _____	Time: _____ OZ: _____

DIAPERS: Today went...

B/M: _____ diapers	Wet: _____ diapers	Combo: _____ diapers

Notes:_____

_____

_____

NAP – TIME: TODAY: Today I slept ...

Start Time: _____	Duration: _____
Start Time: _____	Duration: _____
Start Time: _____	Duration: _____

ACTVITIES: TODAY

Read: _____	□ Went for a walk
Played: _____	□ Went to the Playground
Sung/Danced to: _____	□ Played outside
Learned: _____	□ Watched _____

NOTES

Today my overall mood was: _____

_____

DAILY CHILDCARE LOG

SOLIDS: Today I ate ...

Breakfast Time	Lunch Time
I ate _____ of _____	I ate _____ of _____
I ate _____ of _____	I ate _____ of _____
The meal was: □ yummy □ ok □ yucky	The meal was: □ yummy □ ok □ yucky
I drank _____ ozs of water.	I drank _____ ozs of water.

MILK: Today I drank ...

Time: _____ OZ: _____	Time: _____ OZ: _____
Time: _____ OZ: _____	Time: _____ OZ: _____
Time: _____ OZ: _____	Time: _____ OZ: _____

DIAPERS: Today went...

B/M: _____ diapers	Wet: _____ diapers	Combo: _____ diapers

Notes:_____

_____

_____

NAP – TIME: TODAY: Today I slept ...

Start Time: _____	Duration: _____
Start Time: _____	Duration: _____
Start Time: _____	Duration: _____

ACTVITIES: TODAY

Read: _____	□ Went for a walk
Played: _____	□ Went to the Playground
Sung/Danced to: _____	□ Played outside
Learned: _____	□ Watched _____

NOTES

Today my overall mood was: _____

_____

DAILY CHILDCARE LOG

SOLIDS: Today I ate ...

Breakfast Time	Lunch Time
I ate _____ of _____	I ate _____ of _____
I ate _____ of _____	I ate _____ of _____
The meal was: □ yummy □ ok □ yucky	The meal was: □ yummy □ ok □ yucky
I drank _____ ozs of water.	I drank _____ ozs of water.

MILK: Today I drank ...

Time: _____ OZ: _____	Time: _____ OZ: _____
Time: _____ OZ: _____	Time: _____ OZ: _____
Time: _____ OZ: _____	Time: _____ OZ: _____

DIAPERS: Today went...

B/M: _____ diapers	Wet: _____ diapers	Combo: _____ diapers

Notes:_____

_____

_____

NAP – TIME: TODAY: Today I slept ...

Start Time: _____	Duration: _____
Start Time: _____	Duration: _____
Start Time: _____	Duration: _____

ACTVITIES: TODAY

Read: _____	□ Went for a walk
Played: _____	□ Went to the Playground
Sung/Danced to: _____	□ Played outside
Learned: _____	□ Watched _____

NOTES

Today my overall mood was: _____

_____

DAILY CHILDCARE LOG

SOLIDS: Today I ate ...

Breakfast Time	Lunch Time
I ate _____ of _____	I ate _____ of _____
I ate _____ of _____	I ate _____ of _____
The meal was: ☐ yummy ☐ ok ☐ yucky	The meal was: ☐ yummy ☐ ok ☐ yucky
I drank _____ ozs of water.	I drank _____ ozs of water.

MILK: Today I drank ...

Time: _____ OZ: _____	Time: _____ OZ: _____
Time: _____ OZ: _____	Time: _____ OZ: _____
Time: _____ OZ: _____	Time: _____ OZ: _____

DIAPERS: Today went...

B/M: _____ diapers	Wet: _____ diapers	Combo: _____ diapers

Notes:_____

_____

_____

NAP – TIME: TODAY: Today I slept ...

Start Time: _____	Duration: _____
Start Time: _____	Duration: _____
Start Time: _____	Duration: _____

ACTVITIES: TODAY

Read: _____	☐ Went for a walk
Played: _____	☐ Went to the Playground
Sung/Danced to: _____	☐ Played outside
Learned: _____	☐ Watched _____

NOTES

Today my overall mood was: _____

_____

DAILY CHILDCARE LOG

SOLIDS: Today I ate ...

Breakfast Time	Lunch Time
I ate _____ of _____	I ate _____ of _____
I ate _____ of _____	I ate _____ of _____
The meal was: □ yummy □ ok □ yucky	The meal was: □ yummy □ ok □ yucky
I drank _____ ozs of water.	I drank _____ ozs of water.

MILK: Today I drank ...

Time: _____ OZ: _____	Time: _____ OZ: _____
Time: _____ OZ: _____	Time: _____ OZ: _____
Time: _____ OZ: _____	Time: _____ OZ: _____

DIAPERS: Today went...

B/M: _____ diapers	Wet: _____ diapers	Combo: _____ diapers

Notes:_____

_____

_____

NAP – TIME: TODAY: Today I slept ...

Start Time: _____	Duration: _____
Start Time: _____	Duration: _____
Start Time: _____	Duration: _____

ACTVITIES: TODAY

Read: _____	□ Went for a walk
Played: _____	□ Went to the Playground
Sung/Danced to: _____	□ Played outside
Learned: _____	□ Watched _____

NOTES

Today my overall mood was: _____

_____

DAILY CHILDCARE LOG

SOLIDS: Today I ate …

Breakfast Time	Lunch Time
I ate _____ of _____	I ate _____ of _____
I ate _____ of _____	I ate _____ of _____
The meal was: □ yummy □ ok □ yucky	The meal was: □ yummy □ ok □ yucky
I drank _____ ozs of water.	I drank _____ ozs of water.

MILK: Today I drank …

Time: _____ OZ: _____	Time: _____ OZ: _____
Time: _____ OZ: _____	Time: _____ OZ: _____
Time: _____ OZ: _____	Time: _____ OZ: _____

DIAPERS: Today went…

B/M: _____ diapers	Wet: _____ diapers	Combo: _____ diapers

Notes:_____

_____

_____

NAP – TIME: TODAY: Today I slept …

Start Time: _____	Duration: _____
Start Time: _____	Duration: _____
Start Time: _____	Duration: _____

ACTVITIES: TODAY

Read: _____	□ Went for a walk
Played: _____	□ Went to the Playground
Sung/Danced to: _____	□ Played outside
Learned: _____	□ Watched _____

NOTES

Today my overall mood was: _____

_____

DAILY CHILDCARE LOG

SOLIDS: Today I ate …

Breakfast Time	Lunch Time
I ate _____ of _____	I ate _____ of _____
I ate _____ of _____	I ate _____ of _____
The meal was: □ yummy □ ok □ yucky	The meal was: □ yummy □ ok □ yucky
I drank _____ ozs of water.	I drank _____ ozs of water.

MILK: Today I drank …

Time: _____ OZ: _____	Time: _____ OZ: _____
Time: _____ OZ: _____	Time: _____ OZ: _____
Time: _____ OZ: _____	Time: _____ OZ: _____

DIAPERS: Today went…

B/M: _____ diapers	Wet: _____ diapers	Combo: _____ diapers

Notes:_____

_____

_____

NAP – TIME: TODAY: Today I slept …

Start Time: _____	Duration: _____
Start Time: _____	Duration: _____
Start Time: _____	Duration: _____

ACTVITIES: TODAY

Read: _____	□ Went for a walk
Played: _____	□ Went to the Playground
Sung/Danced to: _____	□ Played outside
Learned: _____	□ Watched _____

NOTES

Today my overall mood was: _____

_____

DAILY CHILDCARE LOG

SOLIDS: Today I ate ...

Breakfast Time	Lunch Time
I ate _____ of _____	I ate _____ of _____
I ate _____ of _____	I ate _____ of _____
The meal was: □ yummy □ ok □ yucky	The meal was: □ yummy □ ok □ yucky
I drank _____ ozs of water.	I drank _____ ozs of water.

MILK: Today I drank ...

Time: _____ OZ: _____	Time: _____ OZ: _____
Time: _____ OZ: _____	Time: _____ OZ: _____
Time: _____ OZ: _____	Time: _____ OZ: _____

DIAPERS: Today went...

B/M: _____ diapers	Wet: _____ diapers	Combo: _____ diapers

Notes:_____

_____

_____

NAP – TIME: TODAY: Today I slept ...

Start Time: _____	Duration: _____
Start Time: _____	Duration: _____
Start Time: _____	Duration: _____

ACTVITIES: TODAY

Read: _____	□ Went for a walk
Played: _____	□ Went to the Playground
Sung/Danced to: _____	□ Played outside
Learned: _____	□ Watched _____

NOTES

Today my overall mood was: _____

_____

DAILY CHILDCARE LOG

SOLIDS: Today I ate ...

Breakfast Time	Lunch Time
I ate _____ of _____	I ate _____ of _____
I ate _____ of _____	I ate _____ of _____
The meal was: ☐ yummy ☐ ok ☐ yucky	The meal was: ☐ yummy ☐ ok ☐ yucky
I drank _____ ozs of water.	I drank _____ ozs of water.

MILK: Today I drank ...

Time: _____ OZ: _____	Time: _____ OZ: _____
Time: _____ OZ: _____	Time: _____ OZ: _____
Time: _____ OZ: _____	Time: _____ OZ: _____

DIAPERS: Today went...

B/M: _____ diapers	Wet: _____ diapers	Combo: _____ diapers

Notes:_____

_____

_____

NAP – TIME: TODAY: Today I slept ...

Start Time: _____	Duration: _____
Start Time: _____	Duration: _____
Start Time: _____	Duration: _____

ACTVITIES: TODAY

Read: _____	☐ Went for a walk
Played: _____	☐ Went to the Playground
Sung/Danced to: _____	☐ Played outside
Learned: _____	☐ Watched _____

NOTES

Today my overall mood was: _____

_____

DAILY CHILDCARE LOG

SOLIDS: Today I ate ...

Breakfast Time	Lunch Time
I ate _____ of _____	I ate _____ of _____
I ate _____ of _____	I ate _____ of _____
The meal was: □ yummy □ ok □ yucky	The meal was: □ yummy □ ok □ yucky
I drank _____ ozs of water.	I drank _____ ozs of water.

MILK: Today I drank ...

Time: _____ OZ: _____	Time: _____ OZ: _____
Time: _____ OZ: _____	Time: _____ OZ: _____
Time: _____ OZ: _____	Time: _____ OZ: _____

DIAPERS: Today went...

B/M: _____ diapers	Wet: _____ diapers	Combo: _____ diapers

Notes:_____

_____

_____

NAP – TIME: TODAY: Today I slept ...

Start Time: _____	Duration: _____
Start Time: _____	Duration: _____
Start Time: _____	Duration: _____

ACTVITIES: TODAY

Read: _____	□ Went for a walk
Played: _____	□ Went to the Playground
Sung/Danced to: _____	□ Played outside
Learned: _____	□ Watched _____

NOTES

Today my overall mood was: _____

_____

DAILY CHILDCARE LOG

SOLIDS: Today I ate …

Breakfast Time	Lunch Time
I ate _____ of _____	I ate _____ of _____
I ate _____ of _____	I ate _____ of _____
The meal was: ☐ yummy ☐ ok ☐ yucky	The meal was: ☐ yummy ☐ ok ☐ yucky
I drank _____ ozs of water.	I drank _____ ozs of water.

MILK: Today I drank …

Time: _____ OZ: _____	Time: _____ OZ: _____
Time: _____ OZ: _____	Time: _____ OZ: _____
Time: _____ OZ: _____	Time: _____ OZ: _____

DIAPERS: Today went…

B/M: _____ diapers	Wet: _____ diapers	Combo: _____ diapers

Notes:_____

_____

_____

NAP – TIME: TODAY: Today I slept …

Start Time: _____	Duration: _____
Start Time: _____	Duration: _____
Start Time: _____	Duration: _____

ACTVITIES: TODAY

Read: _____	☐ Went for a walk
Played: _____	☐ Went to the Playground
Sung/Danced to: _____	☐ Played outside
Learned: _____	☐ Watched _____

NOTES

Today my overall mood was: _____

_____

DAILY CHILDCARE LOG

SOLIDS: Today I ate ...	
Breakfast Time	Lunch Time
I ate _____ of _____	I ate _____ of _____
I ate _____ of _____	I ate _____ of _____
The meal was: □ yummy □ ok □ yucky	The meal was: □ yummy □ ok □ yucky
I drank _____ ozs of water.	I drank _____ ozs of water.

MILK: Today I drank ...			
Time: _____	OZ: _____	Time: _____	OZ: _____
Time: _____	OZ: _____	Time: _____	OZ: _____
Time: _____	OZ: _____	Time: _____	OZ: _____

DIAPERS: Today went...		
B/M: _____ diapers	Wet: _____ diapers	Combo: _____ diapers
Notes:_____ _____ _____		

NAP – TIME: TODAY: Today I slept ...

Start Time: _____	Duration: _____
Start Time: _____	Duration: _____
Start Time: _____	Duration: _____

ACTVITIES: TODAY	
Read: _____	□ Went for a walk
Played: _____	□ Went to the Playground
Sung/Danced to: _____	□ Played outside
Learned: _____	□ Watched _____

NOTES
Today my overall mood was: _____ _____

DAILY CHILDCARE LOG

SOLIDS: Today I ate …

Breakfast Time	Lunch Time
I ate _____ of _____	I ate _____ of _____
I ate _____ of _____	I ate _____ of _____
The meal was: □ yummy □ ok □ yucky	The meal was: □ yummy □ ok □ yucky
I drank _____ ozs of water.	I drank _____ ozs of water.

MILK: Today I drank …

Time: _____ OZ: _____	Time: _____ OZ: _____
Time: _____ OZ: _____	Time: _____ OZ: _____
Time: _____ OZ: _____	Time: _____ OZ: _____

DIAPERS: Today went…

B/M: _____ diapers	Wet: _____ diapers	Combo: _____ diapers

Notes:_____

_____

_____

NAP – TIME: TODAY: Today I slept …

Start Time: _____	Duration: _____
Start Time: _____	Duration: _____
Start Time: _____	Duration: _____

ACTVITIES: TODAY

Read: _____	□ Went for a walk
Played: _____	□ Went to the Playground
Sung/Danced to: _____	□ Played outside
Learned: _____	□ Watched _____

NOTES

Today my overall mood was: _____

_____

DAILY CHILDCARE LOG

SOLIDS: Today I ate ...

Breakfast Time	Lunch Time
I ate _____ of _____	I ate _____ of _____
I ate _____ of _____	I ate _____ of _____
The meal was: ☐ yummy ☐ ok ☐ yucky	The meal was: ☐ yummy ☐ ok ☐ yucky
I drank _____ ozs of water.	I drank _____ ozs of water.

MILK: Today I drank ...

Time: _____ OZ: _____	Time: _____ OZ: _____
Time: _____ OZ: _____	Time: _____ OZ: _____
Time: _____ OZ: _____	Time: _____ OZ: _____

DIAPERS: Today went...

B/M: _____ diapers	Wet: _____ diapers	Combo: _____ diapers

Notes:_____

_____

_____

NAP – TIME: TODAY: Today I slept ...

Start Time: _____	Duration: _____
Start Time: _____	Duration: _____
Start Time: _____	Duration: _____

ACTVITIES: TODAY

Read: _____	☐ Went for a walk
Played: _____	☐ Went to the Playground
Sung/Danced to: _____	☐ Played outside
Learned: _____	☐ Watched _____

NOTES

Today my overall mood was: _____

_____

DAILY CHILDCARE LOG

SOLIDS: Today I ate ...

Breakfast Time	Lunch Time
I ate _____ of _____	I ate _____ of _____
I ate _____ of _____	I ate _____ of _____
The meal was: □ yummy □ ok □ yucky	The meal was: □ yummy □ ok □ yucky
I drank _____ ozs of water.	I drank _____ ozs of water.

MILK: Today I drank ...

Time: _____ OZ: _____	Time: _____ OZ: _____
Time: _____ OZ: _____	Time: _____ OZ: _____
Time: _____ OZ: _____	Time: _____ OZ: _____

DIAPERS: Today went...

B/M: _____ diapers	Wet: _____ diapers	Combo: _____ diapers

Notes:_____

_____

_____

NAP – TIME: TODAY: Today I slept ...

Start Time: _____	Duration: _____
Start Time: _____	Duration: _____
Start Time: _____	Duration: _____

ACTVITIES: TODAY

Read: _____	□ Went for a walk
Played: _____	□ Went to the Playground
Sung/Danced to: _____	□ Played outside
Learned: _____	□ Watched _____

NOTES

Today my overall mood was: _____

_____

DAILY CHILDCARE LOG

SOLIDS: Today I ate ...

Breakfast Time	Lunch Time
I ate _____ of _____	I ate _____ of _____
I ate _____ of _____	I ate _____ of _____
The meal was: □ yummy □ ok □ yucky	The meal was: □ yummy □ ok □ yucky
I drank _____ ozs of water.	I drank _____ ozs of water.

MILK: Today I drank ...

Time: _____ OZ: _____	Time: _____ OZ: _____
Time: _____ OZ: _____	Time: _____ OZ: _____
Time: _____ OZ: _____	Time: _____ OZ: _____

DIAPERS: Today went...

B/M: _____ diapers	Wet: _____ diapers	Combo: _____ diapers

Notes:_____

_____

_____

NAP – TIME: TODAY: Today I slept ...

Start Time: _____	Duration: _____
Start Time: _____	Duration: _____
Start Time: _____	Duration: _____

ACTVITIES: TODAY

Read: _____	□ Went for a walk
Played: _____	□ Went to the Playground
Sung/Danced to: _____	□ Played outside
Learned: _____	□ Watched _____

NOTES

Today my overall mood was: _____

_____

DAILY CHILDCARE LOG

SOLIDS: Today I ate ...

Breakfast Time	Lunch Time
I ate _____ of _____	I ate _____ of _____
I ate _____ of _____	I ate _____ of _____
The meal was: ☐ yummy ☐ ok ☐ yucky	The meal was: ☐ yummy ☐ ok ☐ yucky
I drank _____ ozs of water.	I drank _____ ozs of water.

MILK: Today I drank ...

Time: _____ OZ: _____	Time: _____ OZ: _____
Time: _____ OZ: _____	Time: _____ OZ: _____
Time: _____ OZ: _____	Time: _____ OZ: _____

DIAPERS: Today went...

B/M: _____ diapers	Wet: _____ diapers	Combo: _____ diapers

Notes:_____

_____

_____

NAP – TIME: TODAY: Today I slept ...

Start Time: _____	Duration: _____
Start Time: _____	Duration: _____
Start Time: _____	Duration: _____

ACTVITIES: TODAY

Read: _____	☐ Went for a walk
Played: _____	☐ Went to the Playground
Sung/Danced to: _____	☐ Played outside
Learned: _____	☐ Watched _____

NOTES

Today my overall mood was: _____

_____

DAILY CHILDCARE LOG

SOLIDS: Today I ate ...

Breakfast Time	Lunch Time
I ate _____ of _____	I ate _____ of _____
I ate _____ of _____	I ate _____ of _____
The meal was: □ yummy □ ok □ yucky	The meal was: □ yummy □ ok □ yucky
I drank _____ ozs of water.	I drank _____ ozs of water.

MILK: Today I drank ...

Time: _____ OZ: _____	Time: _____ OZ: _____
Time: _____ OZ: _____	Time: _____ OZ: _____
Time: _____ OZ: _____	Time: _____ OZ: _____

DIAPERS: Today went...

B/M: _____ diapers	Wet: _____ diapers	Combo: _____ diapers

Notes:_____

_____

_____

NAP – TIME: TODAY: Today I slept ...

Start Time: _____	Duration: _____
Start Time: _____	Duration: _____
Start Time: _____	Duration: _____

ACTVITIES: TODAY

Read: _____	□ Went for a walk
Played: _____	□ Went to the Playground
Sung/Danced to: _____	□ Played outside
Learned: _____	□ Watched _____

NOTES

Today my overall mood was: _____

_____

DAILY CHILDCARE LOG

SOLIDS: Today I ate …

Breakfast Time	Lunch Time
I ate _____ of _____	I ate _____ of _____
I ate _____ of _____	I ate _____ of _____
The meal was: □ yummy □ ok □ yucky	The meal was: □ yummy □ ok □ yucky
I drank _____ ozs of water.	I drank _____ ozs of water.

MILK: Today I drank …

Time: _____ OZ: _____	Time: _____ OZ: _____
Time: _____ OZ: _____	Time: _____ OZ: _____
Time: _____ OZ: _____	Time: _____ OZ: _____

DIAPERS: Today went…

B/M: _____ diapers	Wet: _____ diapers	Combo: _____ diapers

Notes:_____

_____

_____

NAP – TIME: TODAY: Today I slept …

Start Time: _____	Duration: _____
Start Time: _____	Duration: _____
Start Time: _____	Duration: _____

ACTVITIES: TODAY

Read: _____	□ Went for a walk
Played: _____	□ Went to the Playground
Sung/Danced to: _____	□ Played outside
Learned: _____	□ Watched _____

NOTES

Today my overall mood was: _____

_____

DAILY CHILDCARE LOG

SOLIDS: Today I ate ...

Breakfast Time	Lunch Time
I ate _____ of _____	I ate _____ of _____
I ate _____ of _____	I ate _____ of _____
The meal was: □ yummy □ ok □ yucky	The meal was: □ yummy □ ok □ yucky
I drank _____ ozs of water.	I drank _____ ozs of water.

MILK: Today I drank ...

Time: _____ OZ: _____	Time: _____ OZ: _____
Time: _____ OZ: _____	Time: _____ OZ: _____
Time: _____ OZ: _____	Time: _____ OZ: _____

DIAPERS: Today went...

B/M: _____ diapers	Wet: _____ diapers	Combo: _____ diapers

Notes:_____

_____

_____

NAP – TIME: TODAY: Today I slept ...

Start Time: _____	Duration: _____
Start Time: _____	Duration: _____
Start Time: _____	Duration: _____

ACTVITIES: TODAY

Read: _____	□ Went for a walk
Played: _____	□ Went to the Playground
Sung/Danced to: _____	□ Played outside
Learned: _____	□ Watched _____

NOTES

Today my overall mood was: _____

_____

DAILY CHILDCARE LOG

SOLIDS: Today I ate ...

Breakfast Time	Lunch Time
I ate _____ of _____	I ate _____ of _____
I ate _____ of _____	I ate _____ of _____
The meal was: □ yummy □ ok □ yucky	The meal was: □ yummy □ ok □ yucky
I drank _____ ozs of water.	I drank _____ ozs of water.

MILK: Today I drank ...

Time: _____ OZ: _____	Time: _____ OZ: _____
Time: _____ OZ: _____	Time: _____ OZ: _____
Time: _____ OZ: _____	Time: _____ OZ: _____

DIAPERS: Today went...

B/M: _____ diapers	Wet: _____ diapers	Combo: _____ diapers

Notes:_____

_____

_____

NAP – TIME: TODAY: Today I slept ...

Start Time: _____	Duration: _____
Start Time: _____	Duration: _____
Start Time: _____	Duration: _____

ACTVITIES: TODAY

Read: _____	□ Went for a walk
Played: _____	□ Went to the Playground
Sung/Danced to: _____	□ Played outside
Learned: _____	□ Watched _____

NOTES

Today my overall mood was: _____

_____

DAILY CHILDCARE LOG

SOLIDS: Today I ate ...

Breakfast Time	Lunch Time
I ate _____ of _____	I ate _____ of _____
I ate _____ of _____	I ate _____ of _____
The meal was: □ yummy □ ok □ yucky	The meal was: □ yummy □ ok □ yucky
I drank _____ ozs of water.	I drank _____ ozs of water.

MILK: Today I drank ...

Time: _____ OZ: _____	Time: _____ OZ: _____
Time: _____ OZ: _____	Time: _____ OZ: _____
Time: _____ OZ: _____	Time: _____ OZ: _____

DIAPERS: Today went...

B/M: _____ diapers	Wet: _____ diapers	Combo: _____ diapers

Notes:_____

_____

_____

NAP – TIME: TODAY: Today I slept ...

Start Time: _____	Duration: _____
Start Time: _____	Duration: _____
Start Time: _____	Duration: _____

ACTVITIES: TODAY

Read: _____	□ Went for a walk
Played: _____	□ Went to the Playground
Sung/Danced to: _____	□ Played outside
Learned: _____	□ Watched _____

NOTES

Today my overall mood was: _____

_____

DAILY CHILDCARE LOG

SOLIDS: Today I ate …

Breakfast Time	Lunch Time
I ate _____ of _____	I ate _____ of _____
I ate _____ of _____	I ate _____ of _____
The meal was: ☐ yummy ☐ ok ☐ yucky	The meal was: ☐ yummy ☐ ok ☐ yucky
I drank _____ ozs of water.	I drank _____ ozs of water.

MILK: Today I drank …

Time: _____ OZ: _____	Time: _____ OZ: _____
Time: _____ OZ: _____	Time: _____ OZ: _____
Time: _____ OZ: _____	Time: _____ OZ: _____

DIAPERS: Today went…

B/M: _____ diapers	Wet: _____ diapers	Combo: _____ diapers

Notes:_____

_____

_____

NAP – TIME: TODAY: Today I slept …

Start Time: _____	Duration: _____
Start Time: _____	Duration: _____
Start Time: _____	Duration: _____

ACTVITIES: TODAY

Read: _____	☐ Went for a walk
Played: _____	☐ Went to the Playground
Sung/Danced to: _____	☐ Played outside
Learned: _____	☐ Watched _____

NOTES

Today my overall mood was: _____

_____

DAILY CHILDCARE LOG

SOLIDS: Today I ate ...

Breakfast Time	Lunch Time
I ate _____ of _____	I ate _____ of _____
I ate _____ of _____	I ate _____ of _____
The meal was: □ yummy □ ok □ yucky	The meal was: □ yummy □ ok □ yucky
I drank _____ ozs of water.	I drank _____ ozs of water.

MILK: Today I drank ...

Time: _____ OZ: _____	Time: _____ OZ: _____
Time: _____ OZ: _____	Time: _____ OZ: _____
Time: _____ OZ: _____	Time: _____ OZ: _____

DIAPERS: Today went...

B/M: _____ diapers	Wet: _____ diapers	Combo: _____ diapers

Notes:_____

_____

_____

NAP – TIME: TODAY: Today I slept ...

Start Time: _____	Duration: _____
Start Time: _____	Duration: _____
Start Time: _____	Duration: _____

ACTVITIES: TODAY

Read: _____	□ Went for a walk
Played: _____	□ Went to the Playground
Sung/Danced to: _____	□ Played outside
Learned: _____	□ Watched _____

NOTES

Today my overall mood was: _____

_____

DAILY CHILDCARE LOG

SOLIDS: Today I ate ...

Breakfast Time	Lunch Time
I ate _____ of _____	I ate _____ of _____
I ate _____ of _____	I ate _____ of _____
The meal was: ☐ yummy ☐ ok ☐ yucky	The meal was: ☐ yummy ☐ ok ☐ yucky
I drank _____ ozs of water.	I drank _____ ozs of water.

MILK: Today I drank ...

Time: _____ OZ: _____	Time: _____ OZ: _____
Time: _____ OZ: _____	Time: _____ OZ: _____
Time: _____ OZ: _____	Time: _____ OZ: _____

DIAPERS: Today went...

B/M: _____ diapers	Wet: _____ diapers	Combo: _____ diapers

Notes:_____

_____

_____

NAP – TIME: TODAY: Today I slept ...

Start Time: _____	Duration: _____
Start Time: _____	Duration: _____
Start Time: _____	Duration: _____

ACTVITIES: TODAY

Read: _____	☐ Went for a walk
Played: _____	☐ Went to the Playground
Sung/Danced to: _____	☐ Played outside
Learned: _____	☐ Watched _____

NOTES

Today my overall mood was: _____

_____

DAILY CHILDCARE LOG

SOLIDS: Today I ate …

Breakfast Time	Lunch Time
I ate _____ of _____	I ate _____ of _____
I ate _____ of _____	I ate _____ of _____
The meal was: □ yummy □ ok □ yucky	The meal was: □ yummy □ ok □ yucky
I drank _____ ozs of water.	I drank _____ ozs of water.

MILK: Today I drank …

Time: _____ OZ: _____	Time: _____ OZ: _____
Time: _____ OZ: _____	Time: _____ OZ: _____
Time: _____ OZ: _____	Time: _____ OZ: _____

DIAPERS: Today went…

B/M: _____ diapers	Wet: _____ diapers	Combo: _____ diapers

Notes:_____

_____

_____

NAP – TIME: TODAY: Today I slept …

Start Time: _____	Duration: _____
Start Time: _____	Duration: _____
Start Time: _____	Duration: _____

ACTVITIES: TODAY

Read: _____	□ Went for a walk
Played: _____	□ Went to the Playground
Sung/Danced to: _____	□ Played outside
Learned: _____	□ Watched _____

NOTES

Today my overall mood was: _____

_____

DAILY CHILDCARE LOG

SOLIDS: Today I ate ...

Breakfast Time	Lunch Time
I ate _____ of _____	I ate _____ of _____
I ate _____ of _____	I ate _____ of _____
The meal was: ☐ yummy ☐ ok ☐ yucky	The meal was: ☐ yummy ☐ ok ☐ yucky
I drank _____ ozs of water.	I drank _____ ozs of water.

MILK: Today I drank ...

Time: _____ OZ: _____	Time: _____ OZ: _____
Time: _____ OZ: _____	Time: _____ OZ: _____
Time: _____ OZ: _____	Time: _____ OZ: _____

DIAPERS: Today went...

B/M: _____ diapers	Wet: _____ diapers	Combo: _____ diapers

Notes:_____

_____

_____

NAP – TIME: TODAY: Today I slept ...

Start Time: _____	Duration: _____
Start Time: _____	Duration: _____
Start Time: _____	Duration: _____

ACTVITIES: TODAY

Read: _____	☐ Went for a walk
Played: _____	☐ Went to the Playground
Sung/Danced to: _____	☐ Played outside
Learned: _____	☐ Watched _____

NOTES

Today my overall mood was: _____

_____

_____

DAILY CHILDCARE LOG

SOLIDS: Today I ate ...

Breakfast Time	Lunch Time
I ate _____ of _____	I ate _____ of _____
I ate _____ of _____	I ate _____ of _____
The meal was: ☐ yummy ☐ ok ☐ yucky	The meal was: ☐ yummy ☐ ok ☐ yucky
I drank _____ ozs of water.	I drank _____ ozs of water.

MILK: Today I drank ...

Time: _____ OZ: _____	Time: _____ OZ: _____
Time: _____ OZ: _____	Time: _____ OZ: _____
Time: _____ OZ: _____	Time: _____ OZ: _____

DIAPERS: Today went...

B/M: _____ diapers	Wet: _____ diapers	Combo: _____ diapers

Notes:_____

_____

_____

NAP – TIME: TODAY: Today I slept ...

Start Time: _____	Duration: _____
Start Time: _____	Duration: _____
Start Time: _____	Duration: _____

ACTVITIES: TODAY

Read: _____	☐ Went for a walk
Played: _____	☐ Went to the Playground
Sung/Danced to: _____	☐ Played outside
Learned: _____	☐ Watched _____

NOTES

Today my overall mood was: _____

_____

DAILY CHILDCARE LOG

SOLIDS: Today I ate ...

Breakfast Time	Lunch Time
I ate _____ of _____	I ate _____ of _____
I ate _____ of _____	I ate _____ of _____
The meal was: □ yummy □ ok □ yucky	The meal was: □ yummy □ ok □ yucky
I drank _____ ozs of water.	I drank _____ ozs of water.

MILK: Today I drank ...

Time: _____ OZ: _____	Time: _____ OZ: _____
Time: _____ OZ: _____	Time: _____ OZ: _____
Time: _____ OZ: _____	Time: _____ OZ: _____

DIAPERS: Today went...

B/M: _____ diapers	Wet: _____ diapers	Combo: _____ diapers

Notes:_____

_____

_____

NAP – TIME: TODAY: Today I slept ...

Start Time: _____	Duration: _____
Start Time: _____	Duration: _____
Start Time: _____	Duration: _____

ACTVITIES: TODAY

Read: _____	□ Went for a walk
Played: _____	□ Went to the Playground
Sung/Danced to: _____	□ Played outside
Learned: _____	□ Watched _____

NOTES

Today my overall mood was: _____

_____

DAILY CHILDCARE LOG

SOLIDS: Today I ate ...

Breakfast Time	Lunch Time
I ate _____ of _____	I ate _____ of _____
I ate _____ of _____	I ate _____ of _____
The meal was: ☐ yummy ☐ ok ☐ yucky	The meal was: ☐ yummy ☐ ok ☐ yucky
I drank _____ ozs of water.	I drank _____ ozs of water.

MILK: Today I drank ...

Time: _____ OZ: _____	Time: _____ OZ: _____
Time: _____ OZ: _____	Time: _____ OZ: _____
Time: _____ OZ: _____	Time: _____ OZ: _____

DIAPERS: Today went...

B/M: _____ diapers	Wet: _____ diapers	Combo: _____ diapers

Notes:_____

_____

_____

NAP – TIME: TODAY: Today I slept ...

Start Time: _____	Duration: _____
Start Time: _____	Duration: _____
Start Time: _____	Duration: _____

ACTVITIES: TODAY

Read: _____	☐ Went for a walk
Played: _____	☐ Went to the Playground
Sung/Danced to: _____	☐ Played outside
Learned: _____	☐ Watched _____

NOTES

Today my overall mood was: _____

_____

DAILY CHILDCARE LOG

SOLIDS: Today I ate …

Breakfast Time	Lunch Time
I ate _____ of _____	I ate _____ of _____
I ate _____ of _____	I ate _____ of _____
The meal was: □ yummy □ ok □ yucky	The meal was: □ yummy □ ok □ yucky
I drank _____ ozs of water.	I drank _____ ozs of water.

MILK: Today I drank …

Time: _____ OZ: _____	Time: _____ OZ: _____
Time: _____ OZ: _____	Time: _____ OZ: _____
Time: _____ OZ: _____	Time: _____ OZ: _____

DIAPERS: Today went…

B/M: _____ diapers	Wet: _____ diapers	Combo: _____ diapers

Notes:_____

_____

_____

NAP – TIME: TODAY: Today I slept …

Start Time: _____	Duration: _____
Start Time: _____	Duration: _____
Start Time: _____	Duration: _____

ACTVITIES: TODAY

Read: _____	□ Went for a walk
Played: _____	□ Went to the Playground
Sung/Danced to: _____	□ Played outside
Learned: _____	□ Watched _____

NOTES

Today my overall mood was: _____

_____

DAILY CHILDCARE LOG

SOLIDS: Today I ate ...

Breakfast Time	Lunch Time
I ate _____ of _____	I ate _____ of _____
I ate _____ of _____	I ate _____ of _____
The meal was: □ yummy □ ok □ yucky	The meal was: □ yummy □ ok □ yucky
I drank _____ ozs of water.	I drank _____ ozs of water.

MILK: Today I drank ...

Time: _____ OZ: _____	Time: _____ OZ: _____
Time: _____ OZ: _____	Time: _____ OZ: _____
Time: _____ OZ: _____	Time: _____ OZ: _____

DIAPERS: Today went...

B/M: _____ diapers	Wet: _____ diapers	Combo: _____ diapers

Notes:_____

_____

_____

NAP – TIME: TODAY: Today I slept ...

Start Time: _____	Duration: _____
Start Time: _____	Duration: _____
Start Time: _____	Duration: _____

ACTVITIES: TODAY

Read: _____	□ Went for a walk
Played: _____	□ Went to the Playground
Sung/Danced to: _____	□ Played outside
Learned: _____	□ Watched _____

NOTES

Today my overall mood was: _____

_____

DAILY CHILDCARE LOG

SOLIDS: Today I ate ...

Breakfast Time	Lunch Time
I ate _____ of _____	I ate _____ of _____
I ate _____ of _____	I ate _____ of _____
The meal was: □ yummy □ ok □ yucky	The meal was: □ yummy □ ok □ yucky
I drank _____ ozs of water.	I drank _____ ozs of water.

MILK: Today I drank ...

Time: _____ OZ: _____	Time: _____ OZ: _____
Time: _____ OZ: _____	Time: _____ OZ: _____
Time: _____ OZ: _____	Time: _____ OZ: _____

DIAPERS: Today went...

B/M: _____ diapers	Wet: _____ diapers	Combo: _____ diapers

Notes:_____

_____

_____

NAP – TIME: TODAY: Today I slept ...

Start Time: _____	Duration: _____
Start Time: _____	Duration: _____
Start Time: _____	Duration: _____

ACTVITIES: TODAY

Read: _____	□ Went for a walk
Played: _____	□ Went to the Playground
Sung/Danced to: _____	□ Played outside
Learned: _____	□ Watched _____

NOTES

Today my overall mood was: _____

_____

DAILY CHILDCARE LOG

SOLIDS: Today I ate ...

Breakfast Time	Lunch Time
I ate _____ of _____	I ate _____ of _____
I ate _____ of _____	I ate _____ of _____
The meal was: □ yummy □ ok □ yucky	The meal was: □ yummy □ ok □ yucky
I drank _____ ozs of water.	I drank _____ ozs of water.

MILK: Today I drank ...

Time: _____ OZ: _____	Time: _____ OZ: _____
Time: _____ OZ: _____	Time: _____ OZ: _____
Time: _____ OZ: _____	Time: _____ OZ: _____

DIAPERS: Today went...

B/M: _____ diapers	Wet: _____ diapers	Combo: _____ diapers

Notes:_____

_____

_____

NAP – TIME: TODAY: Today I slept ...

Start Time: _____	Duration: _____
Start Time: _____	Duration: _____
Start Time: _____	Duration: _____

ACTVITIES: TODAY

Read: _____	□ Went for a walk
Played: _____	□ Went to the Playground
Sung/Danced to: _____	□ Played outside
Learned: _____	□ Watched _____

NOTES

Today my overall mood was: _____

_____

DAILY CHILDCARE LOG

SOLIDS: Today I ate …

Breakfast Time	Lunch Time
I ate _____ of _____	I ate _____ of _____
I ate _____ of _____	I ate _____ of _____
The meal was: □ yummy □ ok □ yucky	The meal was: □ yummy □ ok □ yucky
I drank _____ ozs of water.	I drank _____ ozs of water.

MILK: Today I drank …

Time: _____ OZ: _____	Time: _____ OZ: _____
Time: _____ OZ: _____	Time: _____ OZ: _____
Time: _____ OZ: _____	Time: _____ OZ: _____

DIAPERS: Today went…

B/M: _____ diapers	Wet: _____ diapers	Combo: _____ diapers

Notes:_____

_____

_____

NAP – TIME: TODAY: Today I slept …

Start Time: _____	Duration: _____
Start Time: _____	Duration: _____
Start Time: _____	Duration: _____

ACTVITIES: TODAY

Read: _____	□ Went for a walk
Played: _____	□ Went to the Playground
Sung/Danced to: _____	□ Played outside
Learned: _____	□ Watched _____

NOTES

Today my overall mood was: _____

_____

DAILY CHILDCARE LOG

SOLIDS: Today I ate ...

Breakfast Time	Lunch Time
I ate _____ of _____	I ate _____ of _____
I ate _____ of _____	I ate _____ of _____
The meal was: □ yummy □ ok □ yucky	The meal was: □ yummy □ ok □ yucky
I drank _____ ozs of water.	I drank _____ ozs of water.

MILK: Today I drank ...

Time: _____ OZ: _____	Time: _____ OZ: _____
Time: _____ OZ: _____	Time: _____ OZ: _____
Time: _____ OZ: _____	Time: _____ OZ: _____

DIAPERS: Today went...

B/M: _____ diapers	Wet: _____ diapers	Combo: _____ diapers

Notes:_____

_____

_____

NAP – TIME: TODAY: Today I slept ...

Start Time: _____	Duration: _____
Start Time: _____	Duration: _____
Start Time: _____	Duration: _____

ACTVITIES: TODAY

Read: _____	□ Went for a walk
Played: _____	□ Went to the Playground
Sung/Danced to: _____	□ Played outside
Learned: _____	□ Watched _____

NOTES

Today my overall mood was: _____

_____

DAILY CHILDCARE LOG

SOLIDS: Today I ate ...

Breakfast Time	Lunch Time
I ate _____ of _____	I ate _____ of _____
I ate _____ of _____	I ate _____ of _____
The meal was: □ yummy □ ok □ yucky	The meal was: □ yummy □ ok □ yucky
I drank _____ ozs of water.	I drank _____ ozs of water.

MILK: Today I drank ...

Time: _____ OZ: _____	Time: _____ OZ: _____
Time: _____ OZ: _____	Time: _____ OZ: _____
Time: _____ OZ: _____	Time: _____ OZ: _____

DIAPERS: Today went...

B/M: _____ diapers	Wet: _____ diapers	Combo: _____ diapers

Notes:_____

_____

_____

NAP – TIME: TODAY: Today I slept ...

Start Time: _____	Duration: _____
Start Time: _____	Duration: _____
Start Time: _____	Duration: _____

ACTVITIES: TODAY

Read: _____	□ Went for a walk
Played: _____	□ Went to the Playground
Sung/Danced to: _____	□ Played outside
Learned: _____	□ Watched _____

NOTES

Today my overall mood was: _____

_____

DAILY CHILDCARE LOG

SOLIDS: Today I ate ...

Breakfast Time	Lunch Time
I ate _____ of _____	I ate _____ of _____
I ate _____ of _____	I ate _____ of _____
The meal was: □ yummy □ ok □ yucky	The meal was: □ yummy □ ok □ yucky
I drank _____ ozs of water.	I drank _____ ozs of water.

MILK: Today I drank ...

Time: _____ OZ: _____	Time: _____ OZ: _____
Time: _____ OZ: _____	Time: _____ OZ: _____
Time: _____ OZ: _____	Time: _____ OZ: _____

DIAPERS: Today went...

B/M: _____ diapers	Wet: _____ diapers	Combo: _____ diapers

Notes:_____

_____

_____

NAP – TIME: TODAY: Today I slept ...

Start Time: _____	Duration: _____
Start Time: _____	Duration: _____
Start Time: _____	Duration: _____

ACTVITIES: TODAY

Read: _____	□ Went for a walk
Played: _____	□ Went to the Playground
Sung/Danced to: _____	□ Played outside
Learned: _____	□ Watched _____

NOTES

Today my overall mood was: _____

_____

DAILY CHILDCARE LOG

SOLIDS: Today I ate ...

Breakfast Time	Lunch Time
I ate _____ of _____	I ate _____ of _____
I ate _____ of _____	I ate _____ of _____
The meal was: □ yummy □ ok □ yucky	The meal was: □ yummy □ ok □ yucky
I drank _____ ozs of water.	I drank _____ ozs of water.

MILK: Today I drank ...

Time: _____ OZ: _____	Time: _____ OZ: _____
Time: _____ OZ: _____	Time: _____ OZ: _____
Time: _____ OZ: _____	Time: _____ OZ: _____

DIAPERS: Today went...

B/M: _____ diapers	Wet: _____ diapers	Combo: _____ diapers

Notes:_____

_____

_____

NAP – TIME: TODAY: Today I slept ...

Start Time: _____	Duration: _____
Start Time: _____	Duration: _____
Start Time: _____	Duration: _____

ACTVITIES: TODAY

Read: _____	□ Went for a walk
Played: _____	□ Went to the Playground
Sung/Danced to: _____	□ Played outside
Learned: _____	□ Watched _____

NOTES

Today my overall mood was: _____

_____

DAILY CHILDCARE LOG

SOLIDS: Today I ate ...

Breakfast Time	Lunch Time
I ate _____ of _____	I ate _____ of _____
I ate _____ of _____	I ate _____ of _____
The meal was: ☐ yummy ☐ ok ☐ yucky	The meal was: ☐ yummy ☐ ok ☐ yucky
I drank _____ ozs of water.	I drank _____ ozs of water.

MILK: Today I drank ...

Time: _____ OZ: _____	Time: _____ OZ: _____
Time: _____ OZ: _____	Time: _____ OZ: _____
Time: _____ OZ: _____	Time: _____ OZ: _____

DIAPERS: Today went...

B/M: _____ diapers	Wet: _____ diapers	Combo: _____ diapers

Notes:_____

_____

_____

NAP – TIME: TODAY: Today I slept ...

Start Time: _____	Duration: _____
Start Time: _____	Duration: _____
Start Time: _____	Duration: _____

ACTVITIES: TODAY

Read: _____	☐ Went for a walk
Played: _____	☐ Went to the Playground
Sung/Danced to: _____	☐ Played outside
Learned: _____	☐ Watched _____

NOTES

Today my overall mood was: _____

_____

DAILY CHILDCARE LOG

SOLIDS: Today I ate ...

Breakfast Time	Lunch Time
I ate _____ of _____	I ate _____ of _____
I ate _____ of _____	I ate _____ of _____
The meal was: □ yummy □ ok □ yucky	The meal was: □ yummy □ ok □ yucky
I drank _____ ozs of water.	I drank _____ ozs of water.

MILK: Today I drank ...

Time: _____ OZ: _____	Time: _____ OZ: _____
Time: _____ OZ: _____	Time: _____ OZ: _____
Time: _____ OZ: _____	Time: _____ OZ: _____

DIAPERS: Today went...

B/M: _____ diapers	Wet: _____ diapers	Combo: _____ diapers

Notes:_____

_____

_____

NAP – TIME: TODAY: Today I slept ...

Start Time: _____	Duration: _____
Start Time: _____	Duration: _____
Start Time: _____	Duration: _____

ACTVITIES: TODAY

Read: _____	□ Went for a walk
Played: _____	□ Went to the Playground
Sung/Danced to: _____	□ Played outside
Learned: _____	□ Watched _____

NOTES

Today my overall mood was: _____

_____

DAILY CHILDCARE LOG

SOLIDS: Today I ate ...

Breakfast Time	Lunch Time
I ate _____ of _____	I ate _____ of _____
I ate _____ of _____	I ate _____ of _____
The meal was: □ yummy □ ok □ yucky	The meal was: □ yummy □ ok □ yucky
I drank _____ ozs of water.	I drank _____ ozs of water.

MILK: Today I drank ...

Time: _____ OZ: _____	Time: _____ OZ: _____
Time: _____ OZ: _____	Time: _____ OZ: _____
Time: _____ OZ: _____	Time: _____ OZ: _____

DIAPERS: Today went...

B/M: _____ diapers	Wet: _____ diapers	Combo: _____ diapers

Notes:_____

_____

_____

NAP – TIME: TODAY: Today I slept ...

Start Time: _____	Duration: _____
Start Time: _____	Duration: _____
Start Time: _____	Duration: _____

ACTVITIES: TODAY

Read: _____	□ Went for a walk
Played: _____	□ Went to the Playground
Sung/Danced to: _____	□ Played outside
Learned: _____	□ Watched _____

NOTES

Today my overall mood was: _____

_____

DAILY CHILDCARE LOG

SOLIDS: Today I ate …

Breakfast Time	Lunch Time
I ate _____ of _____	I ate _____ of _____
I ate _____ of _____	I ate _____ of _____
The meal was: □ yummy □ ok □ yucky	The meal was: □ yummy □ ok □ yucky
I drank _____ ozs of water.	I drank _____ ozs of water.

MILK: Today I drank …

Time: _____	OZ: _____	Time: _____	OZ: _____
Time: _____	OZ: _____	Time: _____	OZ: _____
Time: _____	OZ: _____	Time: _____	OZ: _____

DIAPERS: Today went…

B/M: _____ diapers	Wet: _____ diapers	Combo: _____ diapers

Notes:_____

_____

_____

NAP – TIME: TODAY: Today I slept …

Start Time: _____	Duration: _____
Start Time: _____	Duration: _____
Start Time: _____	Duration: _____

ACTVITIES: TODAY

Read: _____	□ Went for a walk
Played: _____	□ Went to the Playground
Sung/Danced to: _____	□ Played outside
Learned: _____	□ Watched _____

NOTES

Today my overall mood was: _____

_____

DAILY CHILDCARE LOG

SOLIDS: Today I ate ...

Breakfast Time	Lunch Time
I ate _____ of _____	I ate _____ of _____
I ate _____ of _____	I ate _____ of _____
The meal was: □ yummy □ ok □ yucky	The meal was: □ yummy □ ok □ yucky
I drank _____ ozs of water.	I drank _____ ozs of water.

MILK: Today I drank ...

Time: _____ OZ: _____	Time: _____ OZ: _____
Time: _____ OZ: _____	Time: _____ OZ: _____
Time: _____ OZ: _____	Time: _____ OZ: _____

DIAPERS: Today went...

B/M: _____ diapers	Wet: _____ diapers	Combo: _____ diapers

Notes:_____

_____

_____

NAP – TIME: TODAY: Today I slept ...

Start Time: _____	Duration: _____
Start Time: _____	Duration: _____
Start Time: _____	Duration: _____

ACTVITIES: TODAY

Read: _____	□ Went for a walk
Played: _____	□ Went to the Playground
Sung/Danced to: _____	□ Played outside
Learned: _____	□ Watched _____

NOTES

Today my overall mood was: _____

_____

DAILY CHILDCARE LOG

SOLIDS: Today I ate ...

Breakfast Time	Lunch Time
I ate _____ of _____	I ate _____ of _____
I ate _____ of _____	I ate _____ of _____
The meal was: □ yummy □ ok □ yucky	The meal was: □ yummy □ ok □ yucky
I drank _____ ozs of water.	I drank _____ ozs of water.

MILK: Today I drank ...

Time: _____ OZ: _____	Time: _____ OZ: _____
Time: _____ OZ: _____	Time: _____ OZ: _____
Time: _____ OZ: _____	Time: _____ OZ: _____

DIAPERS: Today went...

B/M: _____ diapers	Wet: _____ diapers	Combo: _____ diapers

Notes:_____

_____

_____

NAP – TIME: TODAY: Today I slept ...

Start Time: _____	Duration: _____
Start Time: _____	Duration: _____
Start Time: _____	Duration: _____

ACTVITIES: TODAY

Read: _____	□ Went for a walk
Played: _____	□ Went to the Playground
Sung/Danced to: _____	□ Played outside
Learned: _____	□ Watched _____

NOTES

Today my overall mood was: _____

_____

DAILY CHILDCARE LOG

SOLIDS: Today I ate ...

Breakfast Time	Lunch Time
I ate _____ of _____	I ate _____ of _____
I ate _____ of _____	I ate _____ of _____
The meal was: □ yummy □ ok □ yucky	The meal was: □ yummy □ ok □ yucky
I drank _____ ozs of water.	I drank _____ ozs of water.

MILK: Today I drank ...

Time: _____ OZ: _____	Time: _____ OZ: _____
Time: _____ OZ: _____	Time: _____ OZ: _____
Time: _____ OZ: _____	Time: _____ OZ: _____

DIAPERS: Today went...

B/M: _____ diapers	Wet: _____ diapers	Combo: _____ diapers

Notes:_____

_____

_____

NAP – TIME: TODAY: Today I slept ...

Start Time: _____	Duration: _____
Start Time: _____	Duration: _____
Start Time: _____	Duration: _____

ACTVITIES: TODAY

Read: _____	□ Went for a walk
Played: _____	□ Went to the Playground
Sung/Danced to: _____	□ Played outside
Learned: _____	□ Watched _____

NOTES

Today my overall mood was: _____

_____

_____

DAILY CHILDCARE LOG

SOLIDS: Today I ate ...

Breakfast Time	Lunch Time
I ate _____ of _____	I ate _____ of _____
I ate _____ of _____	I ate _____ of _____
The meal was: □ yummy □ ok □ yucky	The meal was: □ yummy □ ok □ yucky
I drank _____ ozs of water.	I drank _____ ozs of water.

MILK: Today I drank ...

Time: _____ OZ: _____	Time: _____ OZ: _____
Time: _____ OZ: _____	Time: _____ OZ: _____
Time: _____ OZ: _____	Time: _____ OZ: _____

DIAPERS: Today went...

B/M: _____ diapers	Wet: _____ diapers	Combo: _____ diapers

Notes:_____

_____

_____

NAP – TIME: TODAY: Today I slept ...

Start Time: _____	Duration: _____
Start Time: _____	Duration: _____
Start Time: _____	Duration: _____

ACTVITIES: TODAY

Read: _____	□ Went for a walk
Played: _____	□ Went to the Playground
Sung/Danced to: _____	□ Played outside
Learned: _____	□ Watched _____

NOTES

Today my overall mood was: _____

_____

DAILY CHILDCARE LOG

SOLIDS: Today I ate ...

Breakfast Time	Lunch Time
I ate _____ of _____	I ate _____ of _____
I ate _____ of _____	I ate _____ of _____
The meal was: □ yummy □ ok □ yucky	The meal was: □ yummy □ ok □ yucky
I drank _____ ozs of water.	I drank _____ ozs of water.

MILK: Today I drank ...

Time: _____ OZ: _____	Time: _____ OZ: _____
Time: _____ OZ: _____	Time: _____ OZ: _____
Time: _____ OZ: _____	Time: _____ OZ: _____

DIAPERS: Today went...

B/M: _____ diapers	Wet: _____ diapers	Combo: _____ diapers

Notes:_____

_____

_____

NAP – TIME: TODAY: Today I slept ...

Start Time: _____	Duration: _____
Start Time: _____	Duration: _____
Start Time: _____	Duration: _____

ACTVITIES: TODAY

Read: _____	□ Went for a walk
Played: _____	□ Went to the Playground
Sung/Danced to: _____	□ Played outside
Learned: _____	□ Watched _____

NOTES

Today my overall mood was: _____

_____

DAILY CHILDCARE LOG

SOLIDS: Today I ate ...

Breakfast Time	Lunch Time
I ate _____ of _____	I ate _____ of _____
I ate _____ of _____	I ate _____ of _____
The meal was: □ yummy □ ok □ yucky	The meal was: □ yummy □ ok □ yucky
I drank _____ ozs of water.	I drank _____ ozs of water.

MILK: Today I drank ...

Time: _____	OZ: _____	Time: _____	OZ: _____
Time: _____	OZ: _____	Time: _____	OZ: _____
Time: _____	OZ: _____	Time: _____	OZ: _____

DIAPERS: Today went...

B/M: _____ diapers	Wet: _____ diapers	Combo: _____ diapers

Notes:_____

_____

_____

NAP – TIME: TODAY: Today I slept ...

Start Time: _____	Duration: _____
Start Time: _____	Duration: _____
Start Time: _____	Duration: _____

ACTVITIES: TODAY

Read: _____	□ Went for a walk
Played: _____	□ Went to the Playground
Sung/Danced to: _____	□ Played outside
Learned: _____	□ Watched _____

NOTES

Today my overall mood was: _____

_____

DAILY CHILDCARE LOG

SOLIDS: Today I ate ...

Breakfast Time	Lunch Time
I ate _____ of _____	I ate _____ of _____
I ate _____ of _____	I ate _____ of _____
The meal was: ☐ yummy ☐ ok ☐ yucky	The meal was: ☐ yummy ☐ ok ☐ yucky
I drank _____ ozs of water.	I drank _____ ozs of water.

MILK: Today I drank ...

Time: _____ OZ: _____	Time: _____ OZ: _____
Time: _____ OZ: _____	Time: _____ OZ: _____
Time: _____ OZ: _____	Time: _____ OZ: _____

DIAPERS: Today went...

B/M: _____ diapers	Wet: _____ diapers	Combo: _____ diapers

Notes:_____

_____

_____

NAP – TIME: TODAY: Today I slept ...

Start Time: _____	Duration: _____
Start Time: _____	Duration: _____
Start Time: _____	Duration: _____

ACTVITIES: TODAY

Read: _____	☐ Went for a walk
Played: _____	☐ Went to the Playground
Sung/Danced to: _____	☐ Played outside
Learned: _____	☐ Watched _____

NOTES

Today my overall mood was: _____

_____

DAILY CHILDCARE LOG

SOLIDS: Today I ate ...

Breakfast Time	Lunch Time
I ate _____ of _____	I ate _____ of _____
I ate _____ of _____	I ate _____ of _____
The meal was: ▢ yummy ▢ ok ▢ yucky	The meal was: ▢ yummy ▢ ok ▢ yucky
I drank _____ ozs of water.	I drank _____ ozs of water.

MILK: Today I drank ...

Time: _____ OZ: _____	Time: _____ OZ: _____
Time: _____ OZ: _____	Time: _____ OZ: _____
Time: _____ OZ: _____	Time: _____ OZ: _____

DIAPERS: Today went...

B/M: _____ diapers	Wet: _____ diapers	Combo: _____ diapers

Notes:_____

_____

_____

NAP – TIME: TODAY: Today I slept ...

Start Time: _____	Duration: _____
Start Time: _____	Duration: _____
Start Time: _____	Duration: _____

ACTVITIES: TODAY

Read: _____	▢ Went for a walk
Played: _____	▢ Went to the Playground
Sung/Danced to: _____	▢ Played outside
Learned: _____	▢ Watched _____

NOTES

Today my overall mood was: _____

_____

DAILY CHILDCARE LOG

SOLIDS: Today I ate ...

Breakfast Time	Lunch Time
I ate _____ of _____	I ate _____ of _____
I ate _____ of _____	I ate _____ of _____
The meal was: □ yummy □ ok □ yucky	The meal was: □ yummy □ ok □ yucky
I drank _____ ozs of water.	I drank _____ ozs of water.

MILK: Today I drank ...

Time: _____ OZ: _____	Time: _____ OZ: _____
Time: _____ OZ: _____	Time: _____ OZ: _____
Time: _____ OZ: _____	Time: _____ OZ: _____

DIAPERS: Today went...

B/M: _____ diapers	Wet: _____ diapers	Combo: _____ diapers

Notes:_____

_____

_____

NAP – TIME: TODAY: Today I slept ...

Start Time: _____	Duration: _____
Start Time: _____	Duration: _____
Start Time: _____	Duration: _____

ACTVITIES: TODAY

Read: _____	□ Went for a walk
Played: _____	□ Went to the Playground
Sung/Danced to: _____	□ Played outside
Learned: _____	□ Watched _____

NOTES

Today my overall mood was: _____

_____

DAILY CHILDCARE LOG

SOLIDS: Today I ate ...

Breakfast Time	Lunch Time
I ate _____ of _____	I ate _____ of _____
I ate _____ of _____	I ate _____ of _____
The meal was: □ yummy □ ok □ yucky	The meal was: □ yummy □ ok □ yucky
I drank _____ ozs of water.	I drank _____ ozs of water.

MILK: Today I drank ...

Time: _____ OZ: _____	Time: _____ OZ: _____
Time: _____ OZ: _____	Time: _____ OZ: _____
Time: _____ OZ: _____	Time: _____ OZ: _____

DIAPERS: Today went...

B/M: _____ diapers	Wet: _____ diapers	Combo: _____ diapers

Notes:_____

_____

_____

NAP – TIME: TODAY: Today I slept ...

Start Time: _____	Duration: _____
Start Time: _____	Duration: _____
Start Time: _____	Duration: _____

ACTVITIES: TODAY

Read: _____	□ Went for a walk
Played: _____	□ Went to the Playground
Sung/Danced to: _____	□ Played outside
Learned: _____	□ Watched _____

NOTES

Today my overall mood was: _____

_____

DAILY CHILDCARE LOG

SOLIDS: Today I ate ...

Breakfast Time	Lunch Time
I ate _____ of _____	I ate _____ of _____
I ate _____ of _____	I ate _____ of _____
The meal was: □ yummy □ ok □ yucky	The meal was: □ yummy □ ok □ yucky
I drank _____ ozs of water.	I drank _____ ozs of water.

MILK: Today I drank ...

Time: _____ OZ: _____	Time: _____ OZ: _____
Time: _____ OZ: _____	Time: _____ OZ: _____
Time: _____ OZ: _____	Time: _____ OZ: _____

DIAPERS: Today went...

B/M: _____ diapers	Wet: _____ diapers	Combo: _____ diapers

Notes:_____

_____

_____

NAP – TIME: TODAY: Today I slept ...

Start Time: _____	Duration: _____
Start Time: _____	Duration: _____
Start Time: _____	Duration: _____

ACTVITIES: TODAY

Read: _____	□ Went for a walk
Played: _____	□ Went to the Playground
Sung/Danced to: _____	□ Played outside
Learned: _____	□ Watched _____

NOTES

Today my overall mood was: _____

_____

DAILY CHILDCARE LOG

SOLIDS: Today I ate ...

Breakfast Time	Lunch Time
I ate _____ of _____	I ate _____ of _____
I ate _____ of _____	I ate _____ of _____
The meal was: □ yummy □ ok □ yucky	The meal was: □ yummy □ ok □ yucky
I drank _____ ozs of water.	I drank _____ ozs of water.

MILK: Today I drank ...

Time: _____ OZ: _____	Time: _____ OZ: _____
Time: _____ OZ: _____	Time: _____ OZ: _____
Time: _____ OZ: _____	Time: _____ OZ: _____

DIAPERS: Today went...

B/M: _____ diapers	Wet: _____ diapers	Combo: _____ diapers

Notes:_____

_____

_____

NAP – TIME: TODAY: Today I slept ...

Start Time: _____	Duration: _____
Start Time: _____	Duration: _____
Start Time: _____	Duration: _____

ACTVITIES: TODAY

Read: _____	□ Went for a walk
Played: _____	□ Went to the Playground
Sung/Danced to: _____	□ Played outside
Learned: _____	□ Watched _____

NOTES

Today my overall mood was: _____

_____

DAILY CHILDCARE LOG

SOLIDS: Today I ate ...

Breakfast Time	Lunch Time
I ate _____ of _____	I ate _____ of _____
I ate _____ of _____	I ate _____ of _____
The meal was: □ yummy □ ok □ yucky	The meal was: □ yummy □ ok □ yucky
I drank _____ ozs of water.	I drank _____ ozs of water.

MILK: Today I drank ...

Time: _____ OZ: _____	Time: _____ OZ: _____
Time: _____ OZ: _____	Time: _____ OZ: _____
Time: _____ OZ: _____	Time: _____ OZ: _____

DIAPERS: Today went...

B/M: _____ diapers	Wet: _____ diapers	Combo: _____ diapers

Notes:_____

_____

_____

NAP – TIME: TODAY: Today I slept ...

Start Time: _____	Duration: _____
Start Time: _____	Duration: _____
Start Time: _____	Duration: _____

ACTVITIES: TODAY

Read: _____	□ Went for a walk
Played: _____	□ Went to the Playground
Sung/Danced to: _____	□ Played outside
Learned: _____	□ Watched _____

NOTES

Today my overall mood was: _____

_____

DAILY CHILDCARE LOG

SOLIDS: Today I ate ...

Breakfast Time	Lunch Time
I ate _____ of _____	I ate _____ of _____
I ate _____ of _____	I ate _____ of _____
The meal was: □ yummy □ ok □ yucky	The meal was: □ yummy □ ok □ yucky
I drank _____ ozs of water.	I drank _____ ozs of water.

MILK: Today I drank ...

Time: _____ OZ: _____	Time: _____ OZ: _____
Time: _____ OZ: _____	Time: _____ OZ: _____
Time: _____ OZ: _____	Time: _____ OZ: _____

DIAPERS: Today went...

B/M: _____ diapers	Wet: _____ diapers	Combo: _____ diapers

Notes:_____

_____

_____

NAP – TIME: TODAY: Today I slept ...

Start Time: _____	Duration: _____
Start Time: _____	Duration: _____
Start Time: _____	Duration: _____

ACTVITIES: TODAY

Read: _____	□ Went for a walk
Played: _____	□ Went to the Playground
Sung/Danced to: _____	□ Played outside
Learned: _____	□ Watched _____

NOTES

Today my overall mood was: _____

_____

DAILY CHILDCARE LOG

SOLIDS: Today I ate ...

Breakfast Time	Lunch Time
I ate _____ of _____	I ate _____ of _____
I ate _____ of _____	I ate _____ of _____
The meal was: □ yummy □ ok □ yucky	The meal was: □ yummy □ ok □ yucky
I drank _____ ozs of water.	I drank _____ ozs of water.

MILK: Today I drank ...

Time: _____ OZ: _____	Time: _____ OZ: _____
Time: _____ OZ: _____	Time: _____ OZ: _____
Time: _____ OZ: _____	Time: _____ OZ: _____

DIAPERS: Today went...

B/M: _____ diapers	Wet: _____ diapers	Combo: _____ diapers

Notes:_____

_____

_____

NAP – TIME: TODAY: Today I slept ...

Start Time: _____	Duration: _____
Start Time: _____	Duration: _____
Start Time: _____	Duration: _____

ACTVITIES: TODAY

Read: _____	□ Went for a walk
Played: _____	□ Went to the Playground
Sung/Danced to: _____	□ Played outside
Learned: _____	□ Watched _____

NOTES

Today my overall mood was: _____

_____

DAILY CHILDCARE LOG

SOLIDS: Today I ate ...

Breakfast Time	Lunch Time
I ate _____ of _____	I ate _____ of _____
I ate _____ of _____	I ate _____ of _____
The meal was: ☐ yummy ☐ ok ☐ yucky	The meal was: ☐ yummy ☐ ok ☐ yucky
I drank _____ ozs of water.	I drank _____ ozs of water.

MILK: Today I drank ...

Time: _____ OZ: _____	Time: _____ OZ: _____
Time: _____ OZ: _____	Time: _____ OZ: _____
Time: _____ OZ: _____	Time: _____ OZ: _____

DIAPERS: Today went...

B/M: _____ diapers	Wet: _____ diapers	Combo: _____ diapers

Notes:_____

_____

_____

NAP – TIME: TODAY: Today I slept ...

Start Time: _____	Duration: _____
Start Time: _____	Duration: _____
Start Time: _____	Duration: _____

ACTVITIES: TODAY

Read: _____	☐ Went for a walk
Played: _____	☐ Went to the Playground
Sung/Danced to: _____	☐ Played outside
Learned: _____	☐ Watched _____

NOTES

Today my overall mood was: _____

_____

DAILY CHILDCARE LOG

SOLIDS: Today I ate …

Breakfast Time	Lunch Time
I ate _____ of _____	I ate _____ of _____
I ate _____ of _____	I ate _____ of _____
The meal was: ☐ yummy ☐ ok ☐ yucky	The meal was: ☐ yummy ☐ ok ☐ yucky
I drank _____ ozs of water.	I drank _____ ozs of water.

MILK: Today I drank …

Time: _____ OZ: _____	Time: _____ OZ: _____
Time: _____ OZ: _____	Time: _____ OZ: _____
Time: _____ OZ: _____	Time: _____ OZ: _____

DIAPERS: Today went…

B/M: _____ diapers	Wet: _____ diapers	Combo: _____ diapers

Notes:_____

_____

_____

NAP – TIME: TODAY: Today I slept …

Start Time: _____	Duration: _____
Start Time: _____	Duration: _____
Start Time: _____	Duration: _____

ACTVITIES: TODAY

Read: _____	☐ Went for a walk
Played: _____	☐ Went to the Playground
Sung/Danced to: _____	☐ Played outside
Learned: _____	☐ Watched _____

NOTES

Today my overall mood was: _____

_____

DAILY CHILDCARE LOG

SOLIDS: Today I ate …

Breakfast Time	Lunch Time
I ate _____ of _____	I ate _____ of _____
I ate _____ of _____	I ate _____ of _____
The meal was: □ yummy □ ok □ yucky	The meal was: □ yummy □ ok □ yucky
I drank _____ ozs of water.	I drank _____ ozs of water.

MILK: Today I drank …

Time: _____ OZ: _____	Time: _____ OZ: _____
Time: _____ OZ: _____	Time: _____ OZ: _____
Time: _____ OZ: _____	Time: _____ OZ: _____

DIAPERS: Today went…

B/M: _____ diapers	Wet: _____ diapers	Combo: _____ diapers

Notes:_____

_____

_____

NAP – TIME: TODAY: Today I slept …

Start Time: _____	Duration: _____
Start Time: _____	Duration: _____
Start Time: _____	Duration: _____

ACTVITIES: TODAY

Read: _____	□ Went for a walk
Played: _____	□ Went to the Playground
Sung/Danced to: _____	□ Played outside
Learned: _____	□ Watched _____

NOTES

Today my overall mood was: _____

_____

DAILY CHILDCARE LOG

SOLIDS: Today I ate ...

Breakfast Time	Lunch Time
I ate _____ of _____	I ate _____ of _____
I ate _____ of _____	I ate _____ of _____
The meal was: □ yummy □ ok □ yucky	The meal was: □ yummy □ ok □ yucky
I drank _____ ozs of water.	I drank _____ ozs of water.

MILK: Today I drank ...

Time: _____ OZ: _____	Time: _____ OZ: _____
Time: _____ OZ: _____	Time: _____ OZ: _____
Time: _____ OZ: _____	Time: _____ OZ: _____

DIAPERS: Today went...

B/M: _____ diapers	Wet: _____ diapers	Combo: _____ diapers

Notes:_____

_____

_____

NAP – TIME: TODAY: Today I slept ...

Start Time: _____	Duration: _____
Start Time: _____	Duration: _____
Start Time: _____	Duration: _____

ACTVITIES: TODAY

Read: _____	□ Went for a walk
Played: _____	□ Went to the Playground
Sung/Danced to: _____	□ Played outside
Learned: _____	□ Watched _____

NOTES

Today my overall mood was: _____

_____

DAILY CHILDCARE LOG

SOLIDS: Today I ate …

Breakfast Time	Lunch Time
I ate _____ of _____	I ate _____ of _____
I ate _____ of _____	I ate _____ of _____
The meal was: □ yummy □ ok □ yucky	The meal was: □ yummy □ ok □ yucky
I drank _____ ozs of water.	I drank _____ ozs of water.

MILK: Today I drank …

Time: _____ OZ: _____	Time: _____ OZ: _____
Time: _____ OZ: _____	Time: _____ OZ: _____
Time: _____ OZ: _____	Time: _____ OZ: _____

DIAPERS: Today went…

B/M: _____ diapers	Wet: _____ diapers	Combo: _____ diapers

Notes:_____

_____

_____

NAP – TIME: TODAY: Today I slept …

Start Time: _____	Duration: _____
Start Time: _____	Duration: _____
Start Time: _____	Duration: _____

ACTVITIES: TODAY

Read: _____	□ Went for a walk
Played: _____	□ Went to the Playground
Sung/Danced to: _____	□ Played outside
Learned: _____	□ Watched _____

NOTES

Today my overall mood was: _____

_____

DAILY CHILDCARE LOG

SOLIDS: Today I ate ...

Breakfast Time	Lunch Time
I ate _____ of _____	I ate _____ of _____
I ate _____ of _____	I ate _____ of _____
The meal was: □ yummy □ ok □ yucky	The meal was: □ yummy □ ok □ yucky
I drank _____ ozs of water.	I drank _____ ozs of water.

MILK: Today I drank ...

Time: _____	OZ: _____	Time: _____	OZ: _____
Time: _____	OZ: _____	Time: _____	OZ: _____
Time: _____	OZ: _____	Time: _____	OZ: _____

DIAPERS: Today went...

B/M: _____ diapers	Wet: _____ diapers	Combo: _____ diapers

Notes:_____

_____

_____

NAP – TIME: TODAY: Today I slept ...

Start Time: _____	Duration: _____
Start Time: _____	Duration: _____
Start Time: _____	Duration: _____

ACTVITIES: TODAY

Read: _____	□ Went for a walk
Played: _____	□ Went to the Playground
Sung/Danced to: _____	□ Played outside
Learned: _____	□ Watched _____

NOTES

Today my overall mood was: _____

_____

DAILY CHILDCARE LOG

SOLIDS: Today I ate ...

Breakfast Time	Lunch Time
I ate _____ of _____	I ate _____ of _____
I ate _____ of _____	I ate _____ of _____
The meal was: □ yummy □ ok □ yucky	The meal was: □ yummy □ ok □ yucky
I drank _____ ozs of water.	I drank _____ ozs of water.

MILK: Today I drank ...

Time: _____ OZ: _____	Time: _____ OZ: _____
Time: _____ OZ: _____	Time: _____ OZ: _____
Time: _____ OZ: _____	Time: _____ OZ: _____

DIAPERS: Today went...

B/M: _____ diapers	Wet: _____ diapers	Combo: _____ diapers

Notes:_____

_____

_____

NAP – TIME: TODAY: Today I slept ...

Start Time: _____	Duration: _____
Start Time: _____	Duration: _____
Start Time: _____	Duration: _____

ACTVITIES: TODAY

Read: _____	□ Went for a walk
Played: _____	□ Went to the Playground
Sung/Danced to: _____	□ Played outside
Learned: _____	□ Watched _____

NOTES

Today my overall mood was: _____

_____

DAILY CHILDCARE LOG

SOLIDS: Today I ate ...

Breakfast Time	Lunch Time
I ate _____ of _____	I ate _____ of _____
I ate _____ of _____	I ate _____ of _____
The meal was: □ yummy □ ok □ yucky	The meal was: □ yummy □ ok □ yucky
I drank _____ ozs of water.	I drank _____ ozs of water.

MILK: Today I drank ...

Time: _____ OZ: _____	Time: _____ OZ: _____
Time: _____ OZ: _____	Time: _____ OZ: _____
Time: _____ OZ: _____	Time: _____ OZ: _____

DIAPERS: Today went...

B/M: _____ diapers	Wet: _____ diapers	Combo: _____ diapers

Notes:_____

_____

_____

NAP – TIME: TODAY: Today I slept ...

Start Time: _____	Duration: _____
Start Time: _____	Duration: _____
Start Time: _____	Duration: _____

ACTVITIES: TODAY

Read: _____	□ Went for a walk
Played: _____	□ Went to the Playground
Sung/Danced to: _____	□ Played outside
Learned: _____	□ Watched _____

NOTES

Today my overall mood was: _____

_____

DAILY CHILDCARE LOG

SOLIDS: Today I ate ...

Breakfast Time	Lunch Time
I ate _____ of _____	I ate _____ of _____
I ate _____ of _____	I ate _____ of _____
The meal was: □ yummy □ ok □ yucky	The meal was: □ yummy □ ok □ yucky
I drank _____ ozs of water.	I drank _____ ozs of water.

MILK: Today I drank ...

Time: _____	OZ: _____	Time: _____	OZ: _____
Time: _____	OZ: _____	Time: _____	OZ: _____
Time: _____	OZ: _____	Time: _____	OZ: _____

DIAPERS: Today went...

B/M: _____ diapers	Wet: _____ diapers	Combo: _____ diapers

Notes:_____

_____

_____

NAP – TIME: TODAY: Today I slept ...

Start Time: _____	Duration: _____
Start Time: _____	Duration: _____
Start Time: _____	Duration: _____

ACTVITIES: TODAY

Read: _____	□ Went for a walk
Played: _____	□ Went to the Playground
Sung/Danced to: _____	□ Played outside
Learned: _____	□ Watched _____

NOTES

Today my overall mood was: _____

_____

DAILY CHILDCARE LOG

SOLIDS: Today I ate ...

Breakfast Time	Lunch Time
I ate _____ of _____	I ate _____ of _____
I ate _____ of _____	I ate _____ of _____
The meal was: ☐ yummy ☐ ok ☐ yucky	The meal was: ☐ yummy ☐ ok ☐ yucky
I drank _____ ozs of water.	I drank _____ ozs of water.

MILK: Today I drank ...

Time: _____ OZ: _____	Time: _____ OZ: _____
Time: _____ OZ: _____	Time: _____ OZ: _____
Time: _____ OZ: _____	Time: _____ OZ: _____

DIAPERS: Today went...

B/M: _____ diapers	Wet: _____ diapers	Combo: _____ diapers

Notes:_____
_____
_____

NAP – TIME: TODAY: Today I slept ...

Start Time: _____	Duration: _____
Start Time: _____	Duration: _____
Start Time: _____	Duration: _____

ACTVITIES: TODAY

Read: _____	☐ Went for a walk
Played: _____	☐ Went to the Playground
Sung/Danced to: _____	☐ Played outside
Learned: _____	☐ Watched _____

NOTES

Today my overall mood was: _____
_____

DAILY CHILDCARE LOG

SOLIDS: Today I ate …

Breakfast Time	Lunch Time
I ate _____ of _____	I ate _____ of _____
I ate _____ of _____	I ate _____ of _____
The meal was: □ yummy □ ok □ yucky	The meal was: □ yummy □ ok □ yucky
I drank _____ ozs of water.	I drank _____ ozs of water.

MILK: Today I drank …

Time: _____ OZ: _____	Time: _____ OZ: _____
Time: _____ OZ: _____	Time: _____ OZ: _____
Time: _____ OZ: _____	Time: _____ OZ: _____

DIAPERS: Today went…

B/M: _____ diapers	Wet: _____ diapers	Combo: _____ diapers

Notes:_____

_____

_____

NAP – TIME: TODAY: Today I slept …

Start Time: _____	Duration: _____
Start Time: _____	Duration: _____
Start Time: _____	Duration: _____

ACTVITIES: TODAY

Read: _____	□ Went for a walk
Played: _____	□ Went to the Playground
Sung/Danced to: _____	□ Played outside
Learned: _____	□ Watched _____

NOTES

Today my overall mood was: _____

_____

DAILY CHILDCARE LOG

SOLIDS: Today I ate ...

Breakfast Time	Lunch Time
I ate _____ of _____	I ate _____ of _____
I ate _____ of _____	I ate _____ of _____
The meal was: □ yummy □ ok □ yucky	The meal was: □ yummy □ ok □ yucky
I drank _____ ozs of water.	I drank _____ ozs of water.

MILK: Today I drank ...

Time: _____ OZ: _____	Time: _____ OZ: _____
Time: _____ OZ: _____	Time: _____ OZ: _____
Time: _____ OZ: _____	Time: _____ OZ: _____

DIAPERS: Today went...

B/M: _____ diapers	Wet: _____ diapers	Combo: _____ diapers

Notes:_____

_____

_____

NAP – TIME: TODAY: Today I slept ...

Start Time: _____	Duration: _____
Start Time: _____	Duration: _____
Start Time: _____	Duration: _____

ACTVITIES: TODAY

Read: _____	□ Went for a walk
Played: _____	□ Went to the Playground
Sung/Danced to: _____	□ Played outside
Learned: _____	□ Watched _____

NOTES

Today my overall mood was: _____

_____

DAILY CHILDCARE LOG

SOLIDS: Today I ate …

Breakfast Time	Lunch Time
I ate _____ of _____	I ate _____ of _____
I ate _____ of _____	I ate _____ of _____
The meal was: □ yummy □ ok □ yucky	The meal was: □ yummy □ ok □ yucky
I drank _____ ozs of water.	I drank _____ ozs of water.

MILK: Today I drank …

Time: _____ OZ: _____	Time: _____ OZ: _____
Time: _____ OZ: _____	Time: _____ OZ: _____
Time: _____ OZ: _____	Time: _____ OZ: _____

DIAPERS: Today went…

B/M: _____ diapers	Wet: _____ diapers	Combo: _____ diapers

Notes:_____

_____

_____

NAP – TIME: TODAY: Today I slept …

Start Time: _____	Duration: _____
Start Time: _____	Duration: _____
Start Time: _____	Duration: _____

ACTVITIES: TODAY

Read: _____	□ Went for a walk
Played: _____	□ Went to the Playground
Sung/Danced to: _____	□ Played outside
Learned: _____	□ Watched _____

NOTES

Today my overall mood was: _____

_____

DAILY CHILDCARE LOG

SOLIDS: Today I ate ...

Breakfast Time	Lunch Time
I ate _____ of _____	I ate _____ of _____
I ate _____ of _____	I ate _____ of _____
The meal was: □ yummy □ ok □ yucky	The meal was: □ yummy □ ok □ yucky
I drank _____ ozs of water.	I drank _____ ozs of water.

MILK: Today I drank ...

Time: _____ OZ: _____	Time: _____ OZ: _____
Time: _____ OZ: _____	Time: _____ OZ: _____
Time: _____ OZ: _____	Time: _____ OZ: _____

DIAPERS: Today went...

B/M: _____ diapers	Wet: _____ diapers	Combo: _____ diapers

Notes:_____

_____

_____

NAP – TIME: TODAY: Today I slept ...

Start Time: _____	Duration: _____
Start Time: _____	Duration: _____
Start Time: _____	Duration: _____

ACTVITIES: TODAY

Read: _____	□ Went for a walk
Played: _____	□ Went to the Playground
Sung/Danced to: _____	□ Played outside
Learned: _____	□ Watched _____

NOTES

Today my overall mood was: _____

_____

DAILY CHILDCARE LOG

SOLIDS: Today I ate ...

Breakfast Time	Lunch Time
I ate _____ of _____	I ate _____ of _____
I ate _____ of _____	I ate _____ of _____
The meal was: □ yummy □ ok □ yucky	The meal was: □ yummy □ ok □ yucky
I drank _____ ozs of water.	I drank _____ ozs of water.

MILK: Today I drank ...

Time: _____ OZ: _____	Time: _____ OZ: _____
Time: _____ OZ: _____	Time: _____ OZ: _____
Time: _____ OZ: _____	Time: _____ OZ: _____

DIAPERS: Today went...

B/M: _____ diapers	Wet: _____ diapers	Combo: _____ diapers

Notes:_____

_____

_____

NAP – TIME: TODAY: Today I slept ...

Start Time: _____	Duration: _____
Start Time: _____	Duration: _____
Start Time: _____	Duration: _____

ACTVITIES: TODAY

Read: _____	□ Went for a walk
Played: _____	□ Went to the Playground
Sung/Danced to: _____	□ Played outside
Learned: _____	□ Watched _____

NOTES

Today my overall mood was: _____

_____

DAILY CHILDCARE LOG

SOLIDS: Today I ate ...

Breakfast Time	Lunch Time
I ate _____ of _____	I ate _____ of _____
I ate _____ of _____	I ate _____ of _____
The meal was: □ yummy □ ok □ yucky	The meal was: □ yummy □ ok □ yucky
I drank _____ ozs of water.	I drank _____ ozs of water.

MILK: Today I drank ...

Time: _____ OZ: _____	Time: _____ OZ: _____
Time: _____ OZ: _____	Time: _____ OZ: _____
Time: _____ OZ: _____	Time: _____ OZ: _____

DIAPERS: Today went...

B/M: _____ diapers	Wet: _____ diapers	Combo: _____ diapers

Notes:_____

_____

_____

NAP – TIME: TODAY: Today I slept ...

Start Time: _____	Duration: _____
Start Time: _____	Duration: _____
Start Time: _____	Duration: _____

ACTVITIES: TODAY

Read: _____	□ Went for a walk
Played: _____	□ Went to the Playground
Sung/Danced to: _____	□ Played outside
Learned: _____	□ Watched _____

NOTES

Today my overall mood was: _____

_____

DAILY CHILDCARE LOG

SOLIDS: Today I ate ...

Breakfast Time	Lunch Time
I ate _____ of _____	I ate _____ of _____
I ate _____ of _____	I ate _____ of _____
The meal was: □ yummy □ ok □ yucky	The meal was: □ yummy □ ok □ yucky
I drank _____ ozs of water.	I drank _____ ozs of water.

MILK: Today I drank ...

Time: _____	OZ: _____	Time: _____	OZ: _____
Time: _____	OZ: _____	Time: _____	OZ: _____
Time: _____	OZ: _____	Time: _____	OZ: _____

DIAPERS: Today went...

B/M: _____ diapers	Wet: _____ diapers	Combo: _____ diapers

Notes:_____

_____

_____

NAP – TIME: TODAY: Today I slept ...

Start Time: _____	Duration: _____
Start Time: _____	Duration: _____
Start Time: _____	Duration: _____

ACTVITIES: TODAY

Read: _____	□ Went for a walk
Played: _____	□ Went to the Playground
Sung/Danced to: _____	□ Played outside
Learned: _____	□ Watched _____

NOTES

Today my overall mood was: _____

_____

DAILY CHILDCARE LOG

SOLIDS: Today I ate ...

Breakfast Time	Lunch Time
I ate _____ of _____	I ate _____ of _____
I ate _____ of _____	I ate _____ of _____
The meal was: □ yummy □ ok □ yucky	The meal was: □ yummy □ ok □ yucky
I drank _____ ozs of water.	I drank _____ ozs of water.

MILK: Today I drank ...

Time: _____ OZ: _____	Time: _____ OZ: _____
Time: _____ OZ: _____	Time: _____ OZ: _____
Time: _____ OZ: _____	Time: _____ OZ: _____

DIAPERS: Today went...

B/M: _____ diapers	Wet: _____ diapers	Combo: _____ diapers

Notes:_____

_____

_____

NAP – TIME: TODAY: Today I slept ...

Start Time: _____	Duration: _____
Start Time: _____	Duration: _____
Start Time: _____	Duration: _____

ACTVITIES: TODAY

Read: _____	□ Went for a walk
Played: _____	□ Went to the Playground
Sung/Danced to: _____	□ Played outside
Learned: _____	□ Watched _____

NOTES

Today my overall mood was: _____

_____

DAILY CHILDCARE LOG

SOLIDS: Today I ate …

Breakfast Time	Lunch Time
I ate _____ of _____	I ate _____ of _____
I ate _____ of _____	I ate _____ of _____
The meal was: □ yummy □ ok □ yucky	The meal was: □ yummy □ ok □ yucky
I drank _____ ozs of water.	I drank _____ ozs of water.

MILK: Today I drank …

Time: _____ OZ: _____	Time: _____ OZ: _____
Time: _____ OZ: _____	Time: _____ OZ: _____
Time: _____ OZ: _____	Time: _____ OZ: _____

DIAPERS: Today went…

B/M: _____ diapers	Wet: _____ diapers	Combo: _____ diapers

Notes:_____

_____

_____

NAP – TIME: TODAY: Today I slept …

Start Time: _____	Duration: _____
Start Time: _____	Duration: _____
Start Time: _____	Duration: _____

ACTVITIES: TODAY

Read: _____	□ Went for a walk
Played: _____	□ Went to the Playground
Sung/Danced to: _____	□ Played outside
Learned: _____	□ Watched _____

NOTES

Today my overall mood was: _____

_____

DAILY CHILDCARE LOG

SOLIDS: Today I ate ...

Breakfast Time	Lunch Time
I ate _____ of _____	I ate _____ of _____
I ate _____ of _____	I ate _____ of _____
The meal was: ☐ yummy ☐ ok ☐ yucky	The meal was: ☐ yummy ☐ ok ☐ yucky
I drank _____ ozs of water.	I drank _____ ozs of water.

MILK: Today I drank ...

Time: _____ OZ: _____	Time: _____ OZ: _____
Time: _____ OZ: _____	Time: _____ OZ: _____
Time: _____ OZ: _____	Time: _____ OZ: _____

DIAPERS: Today went...

B/M: _____ diapers	Wet: _____ diapers	Combo: _____ diapers

Notes:_____

_____

_____

NAP – TIME: TODAY: Today I slept ...

Start Time: _____	Duration: _____
Start Time: _____	Duration: _____
Start Time: _____	Duration: _____

ACTVITIES: TODAY

Read: _____	☐ Went for a walk
Played: _____	☐ Went to the Playground
Sung/Danced to: _____	☐ Played outside
Learned: _____	☐ Watched _____

NOTES

Today my overall mood was: _____

_____

Made in the USA
Middletown, DE
02 October 2022

11666633R00071